by

SHEILA BURNFORD

The Incredible Journey

The Fields of Noon

Without Reserve

Without
RESERVE

Sheila Burnford

with drawings by Susan Ross

Without
RESERVE

An Atlantic Monthly Press Book

BOSTON   LITTLE, BROWN AND COMPANY   TORONTO

ATLANTIC–LITTLE, BROWN BOOKS
ARE PUBLISHED BY
LITTLE, BROWN AND COMPANY
IN ASSOCIATION WITH
THE ATLANTIC MONTHLY PRESS

PRINTED IN THE UNITED STATES OF AMERICA

For the little Indian girl,
and all her brothers and sisters
And for my own brother

Owana ne ke saminik. Owashish, kela na? Kakwan ka totumatan?

Someone hath touched me. O child, is it thou? What shall I do for thee?

—from my CREE GRAMMAR

This book was written
in the generous peace of the MacDowell Colony,
for which the author is sincerely grateful.

Contents

1

A Way to the North

"A Reserve is a tract of land set aside for the exclusive use and benefit of the Indians, ranging in size from a few acres to 500 square miles. . . .

*"A Band is a group of Indians who share a common interest such as land, money, or both, and who generally have a common historical association with a traditional village or tribal unit. . . ." ***

The reserves and bands of Ojibwa and Cree people of whom I have written are all in northwestern Ontario. They vary from those "that objectively one might describe as the social and economic back-

* *The Canadian Indian*, Department of Citizenship and Immigration (Ottawa, 1963).

wash of the bush," * around the shores of Lake
Nipigon, to the wild rice harvesters of the Rainy
River region who have successfully assimilated
their age-old industry with the modern consumer's
world, to the unworldly people of the reserve settlements scattered hundreds of miles apart in that
great roadless area of the map between the north
shore of Lake Superior and the shores of Hudson
Bay.

It is these last people with whom most of the
chapters are concerned, because they are indeed the
"last" people in many senses of the word, and because so few of us have had the opportunity of meeting them against their own background. Most Canadian Indians are still cut off from the white, or
non-Indian, world, but mainly because of psychological barriers; these people of the far northern reserves are cut off by geographical barriers, and in an
age of transition they still know little of any world
beyond that of their settlements, the trapline or the
fishing grounds.

There used to be a saying, with an Indian conno-
tation, about "everyone being a chief." Nothing
could be truer of the paleface world that the people
of the bands of Big Trout and Sandy Lake meet, for
they seldom see any representative of it other than

* Selwyn Dewdney, preface to *Legends of My People* by
Norval Morriseau (Toronto, 1963).

those directly concerned with administration or welfare: missionaries, nurses, traders or teachers who
perhaps live there among them, or officials who fly
in occasionally. Be it bishop or priest, school princi-
pal or teacher, Hudson's Bay factor or clerk, all are
either Chiefs or Little Chiefs, *Okima* or *Okimakan*
in the Ojibwa language, and are distinguished by
the appropriate prefix. Thus the fur trader becomes
Ahmik-Okima (Beaver Boss), his clerk *Ahmik
Okimakan;* the superintendent — or agent as he is
still more frequently called — is *Shuniah-Okima*
(Money Boss), etc. The rare visitor who does not fit
into any categorical hierarchy, such as a sociologist
doing fieldwork or a technician at the weather station, is given some other descriptive name, usually
hinging on an obvious physical characteristic or
character trait, in exactly the same manner that we
ourselves tag strangers: ". . . the mousy/nice/
loud/one who looks like a sheep/has a wooden leg/
never says anything . . ." (It always amuses me to
read those newspaper accounts of the — usually
Tourist Bureau-inspired — Campfire Ceremonials
at which some dignitary visiting a city becomes an
honorary blood brother in the local tribe, receiving,
along with his parchment scroll, his new Indian
name. The dignitary could have two heads or stutter
like a machine gun, yet the name is invariably an
extravaganza of flowery irrelevance such as He in

Whom the Spirit of Brotherly Love Shines Like the
Evening Star, or She Who Throws Open the Gates
of the Morning So That . . . etc., etc.) I don't
know what Susan and I were called in private as we
were neither Chief nor Little Chief nor visiting expert. We hoped it was nothing worse than She Who
Makes Pictures and She Who Does Nothing, but
more than likely it was some wickedly apt pin-
pointing of unconscious or hopefully concealed
shortcoming. In public we got something that
sounded like Mizraw and Mizburp, a rather casual
translation of Mrs. Ross and Mrs. Burnford —
which just about summed us up anyway, in the
kind of planned incoherence of our purpose there.
To the Indian people we were at first the two white
matrons, who were inexplicable, unclassable, because they had come, not to exhort or teach, heal,
snoop, pay or persuade, but in peace alone, in
friendly interest, to learn something of their language and life (and hopefully, we might have
added, to pursue our own interests). We were often
just as inexplicable to those white people, mostly of
the doom-and-disaster brigade, who thought that
the Canadian matron's place was in the home, and
not in the back of some Indian beyond, where if you
didn't die of boredom, frost or rabid-wolf-bite, or in
the middle of taking out your own inflamed appen-

dix, you undoubtedly got Things in your hair or
sleeping bag. . . .

In vain to explain to such people that we felt priv-
ileged to be there at all. In the end we didn't bother,
only doing our utmost to ensure that no one who
lived or worked in the North would ever think of us
as a responsibility, a liability or an intrusion. And
once we had proved ourselves, we found that all
kinds of prejudicial barriers dropped, and that
people were almost always helpful and kind, often
going to extreme lengths to produce persons or
things or places that they thought might interest
us.

If there was nothing altruistic in our original purpose of going, I can only say in our defence that,
after an exotic but unvaried diet of paleface *okima*,
expert and official — some of whom must have been
decidedly unpalatable at times — they probably
found us an undemanding change, a taste of normal
plain fare for once. I hope so.

Neither Susan nor I, committing sketches or
words to paper in those days, did so with any idea of
eventual publication, only for our own personal sat-
isfaction and our own records. Much of what fol-
lows here has been lifted straight out of journal,
notes or sketchbook; the rest has been edited or en-
larged or deliberately written for the sake of conti-

nuity. There are no drums beaten throughout the pages, no problems solved. We were, and are, never happier than among the Ojibwa or Cree people on their far northern reserves, and that is all there is to it.

We shall be happier still if our descriptions will do anything towards helping other non-Indians to understand something of the background from which these people are now slowly and shyly emerging, from those "reserves palisaded with psychological barriers which have prevented close social and economic contact between Indian and non-Indian" * into an often bewildering world, and will accept them with friendship and sympathy into the main stream of twentieth-century life.

Long ago I used to sing a children's hymn about ". . . a green hill, far away, without a city wall. . . ." and always felt very baffled that the hymn did not go on to explain just why this poor particular hill was apparently deprived of a wall. It was not until years later that I realised "without" was the same as "outside." I think now in that context of our children of the North, some of whom are already without their reserve, but most of them waiting, sometimes fearfully, for the gates of opportunity and acceptance to open. I hope that in all

* *The Canadian Indian*, Department of Citizenship and Immigration (Ottawa, 1963).

senses of the word we will greet them without reserve.

Nearly a century ago in Nebraska, an even hundred Cheyenne braves rode into Fort Robinson to
make a token surrender. Acknowledging that the
white settlers were here to stay, and that henceforth
this limitless land would be shared with them in
peace, the braves had been promised immediate re-
lease after making their gesture. "I doubt," wrote a
young frontiersman, "if a hundred (white) men
could be found in the West who would be the equal
of that band. They were kept around the Fort for six
months. At the end of that time they were broken in
spirit and broken in health. They could never be the
same again. That's what has happened to the Indian
everywhere." * He was a bitter young man when he
wrote those words, for he had lived among the
Cheyenne and the Sioux and had a great affection
and admiration for them: these people who had been
betrayed were his friends.

He was right when he said that the Indian "could
never be the same again," but I think that if he were
alive today he would have added that "they could be
different," for he was not to know then the incredible acceleration of life that has overtaken man universally, so that no people can ever be the same, but

* George Philip, "James (Scotty) Philip 1858–1911," *South
Dakota Historical Review*, vol. 1 (October 1935).

must learn to adjust and evolve in a lifetime to changes that once would have taken centuries to bring about. And such a pace leaves no time to waste on regrets.

The young man was my great-uncle, James "Scotty" Philip, and although I never met him, for he died before I was born, he is as responsible for this book as Henry Wadsworth Longfellow or Susan Ross, as Salome Eaglestick, Johnny Little Canoe or Kinessa, as Hopless Beardy or Rubina, or all those other pleasantly named people who have recently come to my mind while I was searching back over the years to the start of a journey that is still going on. I was amused to retrace the rambling and inconsequential route which led me up North in the first place, and pleased to realise that that first Indian camp at Whitefish was, indeed, a destination — even though it was empty and deserted when I arrived there. I had not known I was headed that way, and must be forgiven if the journey rambles in the telling too. It all began with the little Indian girl. . . .

We met when I was about four years old, visiting my grandparents in Canada. Although I cannot now remember the details of where or how — it was probably at the Six Nations Reserve outside Brantford — I can remember her vividly across the years. She must have been about the same age, for below the fringe of her short black hair her eyes, much the same colour as my own but set so much more neatly and compactly within their mongolian fold of lid, were on a level with mine. I had a very battered and face-flattened bear with me, inseparable Bertie, who usually wore a checkered smock over his knitted shorts and a cardigan on top of that, all fastening with fiddly loops and tiny slippery pearl buttons so that dressing or undressing him was a laborious process for my clumsy fingers. And no doubt exasperating for the adult onlooker, for I would not trust him to the hands of any would-be assistant: nobody ever laid hands on beloved Bertie unless I was asleep or unconscious. The little Indian girl knew nothing of the white child's laws of *meum et tuum:* she removed him from my grasp almost immediately; but instead of hanging on to his paw with my normal grim-death clutch or angry roar I let him go without a word. She crouched down, laid Bertie on her knee, and then her thin brown fingers flew competently over those impossible loops and buttons and in a trice his clothes were off. It was sheer magic to me, but to keep my end up somehow I pressed a possessive finger on the worn-out fur of his middle and he obliged with his deep baah-ing growl. It would be stretching the recall of a four-year-old's impressions too far to say that she was frightened, yet I still have a feeling that she was, and that it was some time

before she made him growl herself. What I do remember most strangely and deeply was the then in-
definable impression of our two hands together; one
clean, white, and still babyishly chubby; the other
small and dark with thin deft fingers, so that suddenly I felt most unbearably inadequate and wrong.

It was not just my silly, babyish hands, I think,
but *all* of me — from the clean white socks and
shoes, the flower-sprigged smock and knickers that
I undoubtedly wore to my horrible pink skin and
pudgy knees, and the defenceless thin lids of my
straight-set eyes. Effete and somehow repulsive
would be the words I would have used to describe
myself had I known them then. She was so essentially right in this background that I can no longer
remember, with her narrow bare feet, her short dark
— and undoubtedly dirty — dress, beneath which
she wore, as I noticed when she crouched down,
nothing; the slender, compact coordination of her
body, which made her look as though she had been
poured into her warm, well-fitting skin instead of being stuffed any-old-how into some thin inferior material like me. As I send my mind back over the
years, I can still feel the hopelessness and envy that
engulfed me — an envy that sprang essentially from
the revelation that there existed another simpler,
carefree life for four-year-olds, a life where you just
pulled a dress over your head in the morning and

that was that, and the whole livelong day before you. No struggling into vests and knickers that buttoned on to your Liberty Bodice, no sunbonnet strings starchily rasping your chin, or button hooks making their agonising eighteen hole progress up the protesting plumpness of your gaiter, no socks or shoes that you were always either growing into or growing out of. . . . My adult mind supplies these detailed horrors now, but I have no doubt that they were there unconsciously in that despondent little girl who was me so long ago. (And knowing her so well, I have no doubt that she opened her mouth there and then and bawled her protest at the enormity of it all.)

I often thought about the little Indian girl in the years that followed, supplying her image for an Indian child in stories, later on even mildly boasting at school about having an Indian friend. Then one wonderful rainy Sunday afternoon she became more meaningful than ever. Inspired by the genealogical tree of the Kings and Queens of England that opened out at the back of my history book, I decided to make one of my own ancestors, working backwards from me. But it wasn't nearly as easy as it looked: my mother's side of the family were so appallingly prolific that they kept going off the paper and I would have to start all over again. By the end of the afternoon I had not progressed beyond two or three of Grandmother Macmillan's brothers and sisters; and one of her issue, my mother, was showing distinct signs of irritation at being interrupted so constantly for names and numbers. (Michael, Gabriel and Abdiel had been her contribution to one lot of second cousins; and she had snapped Ranter, Rover, Bellman and True for the offspring of Great Uncle Jonathan.) I persevered to the last brother, James, and hoped that he had either died in infancy or not married for there simply wasn't room for any issue. But he *had* married, said my mother, suddenly brightening, he had married a Sarah Larribee, which had caused quite a stir in the family, although she was apparently very beautiful — and she thought there had been several children. Their names? She had no idea — probably something like Running Bear or Minnehaha, she said, for Aunt Sarah was a Cheyenne Indian; one of her sisters was Chief Crazy Horse's wife, she added, as off-handedly as anyone else might say She married a Brown from Pootersville.

I could hardly believe my ears when she assured me that it wasn't more Ranter and Rover information but true; *all these years and no one had ever told me that I had Indian blood in me.* For surely it followed that if those nameless offspring of James and Sarah were my mother's full cousins, then they must be my second cousins? And their children, who

must be about my age, my second cousins once removed? I looked at my mother with a new interest
and respect; but for someone whose first cousins
were Indians she looked disappointingly normal.
Certainly she had the requisite dark brown eyes of
the little Indian girl, but there was nothing oblique
about them; the same fine-boned hands, but her skin
was distressingly fair. I told her this, and to my surprise she denied, and with some asperity, that she
had anything other than good Scots blood within
her veins — Aunt Sarah Philip was an aunt only by
marriage, she said firmly. And she tried to explain
the difference between bloodlines and otherwise. But
although the evidence was there, and beyond genetic
doubt, my romantic ten-year-old mind refused to accept it inwardly. Like many children I inhabited two
worlds — the mundane real one of endless months
away at school, small and insignificant, interrupted
only by brief holidays; and the other imaginary
world where one was everything one was not —
strong and significant, fearless and gallant, nimble
and wise, truthful and not a bit greedy. . . . My
particular other world was a kind of geographical
cross between Tarzan's jungle and the Swiss Family
Robinson's island, and to the inhabitants there I
now added my Cheyenne cousins — all cast from
the same mould as the little Indian girl. I practised
walking stealthily through shrubberies on non-

twigsnapping pigeontoes — asking of course for a
bow and arrows at Christmas — and I read and re-
read *Hiawatha* until I knew it almost by heart. (By
New Year's Day my bow was locked away: I had
stalked the gardener once too often.)

Inevitably with the years my island sank lower
and lower in the horizon until the day came when I
was no longer able, or needed to chart my course
across the seas of childhood to its shores. But my
interest in those legendary cousins remained, except
that now I directed it into reading all I could find
about the Cheyennes, and about the history of the
West which Great-uncle James had hoped to make.
I knew by now that he had prospected for gold and
driven cattle, and had been a scout and dispatch
rider for the American army at Fort Robinson; in
more peaceful times, as a rancher in South Dakota,
he had foreseen the possible extinction of the bison
and had gathered a private herd together against
this eventuality — all this was family history, but
until I had read his letters, and a biography of him
in a historical review, I did not realise what an ex-
ceptional man he was for his time — a time of the
Indian Troubles of 1875–76, and 1879, when few
white men thought of Indians except in terms of
their extermination by hunting them down, or at
best leaving them to dwindle away in barren reserve
land.

He knew them as few white men did, learning
their language and customs, living among them
both before and after his marriage. It was this intimate knowledge that enabled him to assess the dangerous mood of the Sioux warriors at the height of
their Messiah craze, and to predict the rising that
would culminate at Wounded Knee. Governor Mel-
lette, the first Governor of Dakota, forthwith wrote
to General Nelson Miles, requesting a thousand
guns and ammunition. It is a long letter, almost entirely quoting Scotty Philip's opinions, which ends:
"I know Philip well and will take his judgment on
the situation in preference to anyone I know. . . .
He is a *very cool, courageous man. . . .*"; qualities that Philip himself had ascribed often enough to
others — on the other side. He was proud that his
children had such brave blood as that of the Cheyennes. His marriage was one of the happiest; he was
devoted to his Sarah, who was "as faithful and self-
sacrificing a helpmeet as ever dedicated her life to a
husband."

And I, of course, was very proud of Great-uncle
James, proud that I shared *his* blood, and I longed
to have lived in those days. Then of course I grew
up and longed for other more tangible things; the
war came, marriage and children, and I did not
think of him for years. But when the war was over
and when I knew that we were emigrating as a fam-

ily to Canada, he returned in his full romantic glory, filling my head with all kinds of dedicated notions about Canadian Indians; I too would be a "staunch and stern champion of their rights," (even though I hadn't an inkling of what those rights were, and had not even read the Indian Act). As he had loved and respected his Sioux and Cheyenne, and had learned their language and lived among them, so was I all set to love and respect the Ojibwa and Cree in whose country I would now be living, and to learn their language. I looked at a map, and the names of the rivers and lakes and scattered small towns sang like verses from Longfellow: Keewatin, the North Wind, Atikokan, Shebandowan, Kaministiquia, Windigo, Nipigon. . . . I read *Hiawatha* all over again. And as my uncle had roamed and explored his new land through Colorado, Wyoming, Nebraska and the Dakotas, so would I, in a less ambitious way, get to know something of the land between the far shores of Lake Superior and Hudson Bay . . . I was always a dreamer.

It did not take me long to come down to earth, Canadian earth: what had been an inch or two of it on the map in England turned out to be thousands of square miles of trackless wilderness. It was a tough man's world that even my hero — "that splendid form with its great breadth of shoulder, its two hundred and forty pounds of bone and muscle tow-

ering above his fellows with its majestic head
topped off with a broadbrimmed Stetson hat . . ."
— would have thought twice of tackling by himself. The hinterland of Lake Superior was as inaccessible as Outer Mongolia to housewives like me,
with or without a broadbrimmed Stetson hat.

I reset my sights nearer home, to the lakes and
rivers and logging trails of that wild and lovely land
beyond Port Arthur and Fort William, with "the
shores of Gitche Gumee, By the shining Big-Sea-
Water" almost on my doorstep, and Nanabijou, the
Sleeping Giant, stretched across the horizon of
Thunder Bay. In the warm mellow days of the Indian Summer that ended the blazing glory of the
fall, I fell in love with my new land, with its timelessness, its endless quiet peace, its clear heady air.
After twenty years I am still in love with it.

My husband was busy all day with his pediatric
practice, and Joan, who had always helped to care
for the children and house in England, had left her
Sussex village to throw in her lot with us here, so I
had plenty of time for all my projects. The two eld-
est children were now at school most of the day,
leaving only the youngest to look after. The house
was certainly largeish, but as it was in the country,
and we had hardly any furniture, curtains or carpets
(having decided that a boat or a small second-hand
car for me was far more important), there wasn't

much housework to do. Nor did life centre around
the kitchen. We had never as a family known anything other than rationed food with its dull simple
Woolton Pie-type menus, and either we were so con-
ditioned to these or else so excited about things like
unlimited butter and milk, real sausages, or liver for
the asking, that it never occurred to anyone to de-
mand more exotic and time-consuming dishes.

But it did not take me long to find out that the
more casual approach to home and housework of my
native land was not universal. Nor was it accepted
that women — unless eccentric or Amazonian —
might enjoy walking over the countryside by themselves. The horizons of Canadian matrons — or so
it seemed in Port Arthur at that time — were expected to be bounded by their households, families
and social activities; and these did not leave them
much free time to look further. Within these limits,
everyone was most kind and welcoming and
friendly, but no one ever dreamed of breaking out of
purdah to accompany me or some other such rebel
for a day in the bush or out on the lake. So, except
on Sundays, when we were able to make family expeditions, I explored alone, or in the company of the
family bullterrier, who was supposed to drag me
home with my broken leg, ward off maddened bears
or berserk woodsmen, and generally deal with all

the other evils forecast for reckless matrons — evils which I am still waiting to experience.

After all those years of restriction which I had so recently left behind me, all this was rather a depressing revelation, particularly as I had sworn on leaving England that I would not become one of those immigrants who were forever saying, on either side of the Atlantic, how much more desirable things were on the other. This would be our home now, where we earned our living, and where our children would grow up as Canadians. It was clearly up to me to set a civilised example.

So when the winter drove me in at last, with the snowdrifts deep on my bush trails and nineteen miles of ice stretched out to the flanks of Nanabijou, I made a tremendous effort to conform socially and to be as busy as everyone else. For the first time in my life I went to coffee parties in the morning, and hatted and gloved to teas or bridge parties in the afternoon. I attended PTA meetings and Brownie Fly-ups, joined Ladies Auxiliaries and generally helped to run the country. I made curtains for bedrooms and paper carnations for the hospital. I helped everyone in the family with whatever they were doing, and the house had never looked so tidy — nor the family so exasperated. They begged to return to the certainty of Shepherd's Pie or Grandad's Oatmeal Cookies when I tried out thirteen of the recipes (guaranteed foolproof too) that I had collected at one of my parties or meetings; and they obviously could not wait for spring to come round and free the household of this metamorphosed busy-body.

I had not fooled them, and it was no good fooling myself: my heart simply was not in it. By the time the interminably-waited-for northern spring did come around I was beside myself with the futility of such an existence, and my mind felt wizened from the months of centrally heated small talk and president's reports. With the family's blessing and to their relief, I reverted to form; and the bullterrier and I took off once more.

But his company was not really enough; he did his enthusiastic and inquisitive best but he was not mentally stimulating. I did not join those of my exiled compatriots who complained of missing concerts and theatre and stimulating discussion; I was well compensated by wonderful libraries of books, records and films. But I was inwardly terribly home-sick for the climate of my upbringing. I missed the contentious, articulate company of other Elephant's Children, who like me needed the nourishment of what I can only describe as the climate of *curiosity;* who needed to get their trunks down to the root of the matter and find out for themselves. I

realise now that I simply hadn't met them yet; they
were busy, as they always are, happily pursuing
their own line of country. But, at the time, I marvelled that so many people seemed able to live, as it
were, in a forest all their lives, and to die without
ever knowing more of the trees than that they were,
indubitably, *trees*, things that gave shade, or ob-
scured the view, or got chopped down to keep you
warm.

There was a second disillusionment in store for
me — those lovely euphonic names from the land of
Hiawatha that I had pored over on the map in England. They were there all right, every signpost a reminder of the Indian people, with the unexpected
bonus of the great Ojibwa giant, Nanabijou. The
only trouble was that the people themselves were not
in evidence. In the Lakehead they lived in reserve
land across the river, in the "Mission," a rural slum
of wooden shacks, standing — and sometimes only
just — in overgrown yards with the weeds pushing
up through old tyres and littered junk. And they
were in other evidence only when cutting underbrush on the ski trails, or in the magistrate's court
on some charge, usually a liquor one, when the
newspapers always pointedly distinguished them as
"Indian." Or I would sometimes see children playing, too quietly, in the grounds of St. Joseph's Orphanage and Boarding School, like dull-eyed cap-

tive linnets. No one that I ever met was interested in them; nobody had a good word to say for them. As far as I could make out they existed only in the minds of those directly responsible for their administration or welfare. By this time, mindful of my intended role of staunch and firm champion of rights, I knew what their rights were: it seemed there were hardly any. But when I righteously ascended my little soapbox and pointed out all these shortcomings people just looked uneasily bored. Looking back on it now, it is easy to see why, and I am only amazed that they were as polite as they were: a newcomer to a country, almost fresh off the boat, with an English accent to boot, haranguing the natives about wrongs and injustices to Indians in their own country can hardly expect to command an enthusiastic audience.

After a while I came to my senses, realising that it was one thing to talk, and another to do something about it; and that I was not of the stuff to kindle action. As I had no constructive qualifications to offer and had proved to be less a natural mixer or do-gooder than an immigrant housewife with her head stuffed with romantic conceptions, there seemed no hope — or even point — in trying to establish a Great-uncle Jamesian rapport with something that wasn't even there. With a last sad swing of their gleaming braids my hawknosed, high-cheekboned cousins turned and disappeared in silent file over my

horizon, back to join Great-aunt Sarah and the little
Indian girl in some happier hunting ground on that
long lost Swiss Family island.

I felt even lonelier now.

Fortunately at this low ebb Susan Ross hove over
my gloomy horizon, and I was no longer the Cat
That Walked By Itself, but an overjoyed Elephant's
Child who has just met another in the middle of a
desolate jungle and at long last has someone to play
with, someone whose curiosity is as insatiable as her
own. And through her, I met all those others who
had been there all the time if I had only known it.

Susan's children were about the same age as my
own, but that did not deter her from being a professional painter, nor from reading omnivorously,
hunting and fishing. (Nor had she been deterred
even when the twins were crawling around under-
foot.) I first recognised her by a certain refreshing
objectivity in her dealings with a small nephew bent
on the fratricide of an even smaller nephew: "You
should never bang Timothy on the head with a
plank —" I heard her say. There was a pause while
she apparently mulled over the justice of this edict;
then, "Anyway, certainly not a plank with nails in
it," and another pause, for the final summing up:
"Because it's not good for him." It did not surprise
me to learn that her husband was a lawyer.

She had been born here in northwestern Ontario,

and was as much at home in the bush or in a canoe or an outboard on the lake as I had been in my own country on moors and hills and sea; and she had the sharpest eyes out of doors of any white person I ever met. Susan's idea of purgatory, like mine, was a timeless round of tea parties and small talk. We argued interminably and amicably over everything under the sun. And we both had strangely similar degrees of fixation: where I had Great-uncle James and his Indians, she had Uncle Bob and his Eskimos.

Uncle Bob was Robert Flaherty, the father of the documentary film, whose genius gave the world *Nanook of the North*, who had lived among the Eskimos and counted them as his friends; and who had made names like Baffin, Bylot and Belcher sound like the Isles of the Blest to Susan. If some wand-waving fairy godmother had appeared she would have asked only to be set down on one of them with all her painting gear, and perhaps her earplugs in case some Eskimo snored, there to record with pencil and brush as he had recorded for posterity with his camera.

In the meantime we could only dream our separate dreams about the remote North; but as our children grew older we progressed (often with some of them as enthusiastic as ourselves) from winter's chess battles, necessarily fought on alternate home

grounds, to the formation of a puppet group that
gave shows in the city or further afield. In summer
and spring there was the pursuit of mushrooms and
artifacts; fossils and rock hunting followed naturally. We both liked to hunt and often went out after
partridge or duck by ourselves, her husband being
one of those North American phenomena, the Canadian male who does not think guns or boats or all
the paraphernalia of wildfowling beyond the capa-
bilities or enjoyment of women. It was on one of
these trips, to Whitefish Lake, that I first saw the
Indian wild rice harvesters. Somehow or other, even
after my initial disillusionment about the Romantic
Redskins, my imagination must have got to work
again — only to be given another flattening jolt of
reality. Great-uncle James had not prepared me for
the twentieth century: it would be better to stick to
reading *Hiawatha*.

But my little Indian girl was not going to be so
easily suppressed: she returned very vividly and unexpectedly one day. I had been teaching very basic
elementary English for a few hours each week to a
class of emotionally disturbed adults. Most of them
were New Canadians, part of whose rehabilitation
lay in bridging the lonely gap of non-communica-
tion in a new land that had brought many of them to
the hospital in the first place.

Disliking the over familiar stranger who cannot

talk without some form of physical contact — the confiding arm-presser, the sympathetic, and usually moist, hand-coverer, or the emphatic finger-tapper — I have always found it very hard not to jump like a startled rabbit, or look too obviously like a hedgehog at bay. But many lonely disturbed people long for contact, I soon found out; they want to sit very closely, to touch, to hold a hand. No matter how often I went, it remained an exhausting exercise in self-control to appear outwardly equable when this happened. Then one day two young Indian women came to the class. At first they did little but giggle shyly when I tried to find out how much English they spoke. They sat together, removed as far as possible at the end of the table from the rest of the class, and when the time came for them to go back to their ward they slid quickly through the door without any of the prolonged handshaking or arm-holding of the others. Next time I sat down beside one, and when I had finished printing some word for her, she suddenly took my hand. As usual I felt myself tensing — and with added reason this time: for a moment I thought she was going to bite it, for she had had a violent phase not very long ago during which she had seized another inmate's hand and rammed it through a windowpane, cutting both quite badly. But she turned mine over on one small warm paw while the fingers of the other twisted the moss-agate ring on my finger to look at it more closely. I was irresistibly reminded of a young chimpanzee with whom I had walked, hand in hand, one day in Regent's Park, and who had stopped after a while to look closely at my palm, tracing the lines with a dark pink fingernail like some small hairy fortune-teller. Then, even as I relaxed at the memory and looked down, I suddenly saw those two small contrasting hands lying on Bertie Bear's furry stomach so many years ago; and in the same instant knew again the shock of contrast over the size and shape and colour of mine. Even as I thought how repulsive our white skin must seem to brown-skinned people, I realised too that for the first time I had not recoiled; her hand was warm and brown and friendly only, without intrusively seeking reassurance — it was as confiding, as curious, as a young child's, or that engaging little chimp. It was as though some old recognition stirred in me: it felt *right*.

For the rest of the year I taught, I always felt natural and relaxed with the Indian people who came and went in my class, and yet was never able to conquer — inwardly, anyway — this wariness of contact with the others. I daresay there could be a great long-winded psychological explanation for this, but I find it simpler to think that my little girl friend had put a spell on me forever. . . .

This feeling of rapport grew with the years. I liked their snide sense of humour, and their relaxed extempore approach to time was after my own heart. Against a natural background their company was unequalled. Whole days spent in the immobile confines of a canoe on the marshes were infinitely more peaceful and rewarding with someone who never fidgeted around in the hours of frozen waiting, but seemed to maintain an aware stillness indefinitely, (so that one learned to stop fidgeting oneself). And with them there was never any irritating small talk crackling irrelevantly into an enchanted world bounded by reed-heads and sky, that should be filled only with the quintessence of its teeming marsh life, (and so one thought twice before crackling oneself). There was only the movement of eyes to mark something momentous — some untoward rippling of water within the reeds, a distant flight pattern, a spider lowering himself down from the sky on his shining filament: hunter's eyes certainly, but not the sharp predatory eyes of a white hunter — they were truly "seeing" eyes. I used to wish that I could see through them just once, to find out how different the world around must look.

I remember reading once an account of two men who had spent weeks paddling up some endless river, and the comment of one that to their Indian

guides all nature was their living storybook and
newspaper — a never-failing source of interest
and gossip to be commented and speculated, embroidered and elaborated upon. Long after he and
his companion had watched, enjoyed to the full,
and then dismissed from their talk the sight of, say,
a bear cub being cuffed reprovingly by its mother,
the Indians were still savouring it in every detail,
still chuckling over it, as they themselves could
only have done had the bears been human be-
ings, and with all the why and wherefore of circum-
stance and character filled in so that some conclu-
sion could be reached, or punch line delivered. I was
to find this very true (and most satisfyingly so, having a large anthropomorphic streak myself), and
apparently very contagious, for the only entry in my
journal after one of those days on the marsh is a
three page account of a little teal swimming in awed
astonishment round and round the impassive
wooden form of an outsize mallard decoy; and later
I find a description that would have made even Walt
Disney blush of a gleaming white regiment of peli-
cans standing at attention, then presenting their ludicrous beaks with a Guards-like precision towards
us as we paddled by. And if I could be so carried
away by this sight then my guide must have dined
out on it for weeks.

Then there was Tommy — one of three workmen on a tree-planting project of mine. One of the three was of solid Dutch stock, whose talk was mostly of a grumbling personal nature, and whose eyes brightened only at the sight of a bottle of beer; one was a gigantic Finn who said nothing at all and worked like a bulldozer — I doubt if his vision took in anything beyond the end of pick or shovel. The third was Tommy, small and slight, half Cree, half Ojib, who, as a labourer was probably not as worthy of his hire as the other two, but immeasurably worthier to me in other respects. Despite the loss of several fingers on one hand he tied strange magical flies (which he varied from day to hour it seemed according to the portents) from almost anything he happened to have or pick up — a piece of fur, a feather, a rubber band or a snip of pink plastic. He could take his knife to a piece of soft wood, whittling here, slicing there, until suddenly he gently slid the slices open and there would be an intricately carved fan. And he was a mine of information to me on everything that flew, walked or swam. His hands might be digging a hole but his eyes were everywhere. "Eagle," he once said, when I asked him what he was watching, and he pointed it out over the lake. But it must have been half a minute before the black dot materialised for me, and by that time he had al-

ready seen the identifying white feathers of a bald
eagle on its head — and probably the fish in the
beak of the osprey it was harrying. Yet I thought I
had good sight.

The three were quite a study in contrasts. When
they stopped for lunch and the other two had finished eating and drinking, they stretched out and
had a little nap. Tommy, whose lunch had consisted
of a piece of bannock fished out of his pocket and a
drink of water from the lake, invariably vanished
into the bush with my fishing rod and today's lethal
lure. If he did not return — usually late, to the tight-
lipped indignation of the other two — with a nice
cleaned trout for my supper, it was always with
news of something interesting going on in the bush,
evidence of a bear or deer, or a hatch of partridge
chicks. When it was time to down tools and go the
others did so with promptitude, and left in the short-
est possible line between (a) the site and (b) their
car. Tommy was far more likely to walk around by
the shoreline so that he could show me where the
mergansers were nesting on the way. The other two
were hardworking and ambitious, and would undoubtedly get on in the New World; they were only
doing odd jobs at the moment because they were
temporarily laid off at one of the mills. But I always
thought they only existed whereas Tommy lived.

And, as though to bear this out, the trees that he put in looked far more prosperous than the others the following year.

His second name was Fisher and I always remember his genuine amusement, not in any way wry as it might well have been, over how his father had acquired this surname. Apparently he did not speak much English and the recruiting officer — it was during the 1914–1918 war — was having some difficulty filling in the forms: he eventually managed to get something like Matadeus down for the name, then turned to the other details, but Tommy's father kept insisting "Ochoyk, *Ochoyk*," which the recruiting officer probably thought was his religious denomination or something, for he asked him what it meant in English. "Fisher," said Tommy's father. "*Fisher?*" said the officer. "Fisher, Ochoyk — *me!*" said Tommy's father, patiently pointing at himself, then using his hands to give a graphic description of a fisher jumping off the desk, and finally pointing at his name on the paper (Tommy's own account of this was one of the funniest things I have seen). Eventually light — of a kind — dawned, and the officer filled in Matadeus's surname, and with that Mr. Matadeus Ochoyk vanished and became Private M. Fisher for the duration of the war. After that it seemed better to let sleeping Ochoyks lie forever unchanged, for Mr. M. Fisher was now receiving a wound pension from a grateful government, and Thomas Fisher was written on the birth certificate of his son.

But encounters like these were few and far between; and we spent years filling in the background of that beautiful land of Nokomis, Paunechauk, Kenybeeks and Nanabijou with knowledge about almost everything except its aboriginal inhabitants. Susan and I now fastened inquiring trunks around geologist's picks, now snuffed at wild flowers — and many of the latter ended up in the cooking pot, along with roots, or bulrush heads, ferns and bulbs, for I had found a book listing the Indian uses of many such things, not only as food, but as medicaments. We still dreamed dreams of following in avuncular footsteps, but Uncle Bob seemed to be winning out over Great-uncle James, even for me, for our dreams were mainly of Getting Up North, beyond even Hudson Bay. This was about the time when Eskimo art and soapstone sculpture started appearing on the market through the enterprise of native cooperatives; and Robert Flaherty's name was even more frequently mentioned as public interest in the Eskimos awoke. We longed to go there before spontaneity was lost in a shrinking world. We are still longing. . . .

All this time Susan had painted continuously of course, and I envied her above all things this ability to express herself. Then one day, triggered off by a puppet play or script that had to be written, I started to write. And with the first piece published, with the sight of my own words, I became a kind of print addict and could not stop. I wrote thousands of words about everything under the sun in northwestern Ontario and sent them off to the *Times* or the Glasgow *Herald* — having discovered that newspapers were the quickest way of appeasing my addiction. From then on it seemed that things suddenly started to get under weigh, and for both of us. I wanted to and did write a book, using the rice harvesters as part of the background, and the old interest revived. Susan's paintings of these Indians were receiving much attention, and we went further afield in search of material, to Lake Nipigon.

But still the land North seemed as inaccessible as ever. Then I returned from an unexpected visit to a Hopi Indian reservation in Arizona, burning with new zeal and an interest in contrasting life there with our own Ojibwa and Cree culture; and just then, Election Day rolled around in Canada . . . A banal enough statement, and results themselves did not affect my way of life, but ballot boxes have to be flown to far northern reserves, and somebody in a position of responsibility must accompany them: Susan's husband was now a Judge. There was a spare seat on the aircraft — Susan accompanied the

Judge. And once there, of course, she was determined to find out if, and how, we could return un-
officially, unaccompanied, and stay for a length of
time — instead of just touching down at various
settlements as she had been constrained to do on this
trip. She returned as full of excitement and enthusiasm as I was over my Hopi Indian trip; and with
her she brought, not only a bulging portfolio of
sketches, but the firm promise of a roof over our
heads in the Big Trout settlement if we could get
ourselves up there. . . .

After all these years, and by a route as rambling
and inconsequential as this chapter, we were really
off. . . . I can't even remember now who won the
Election.

2

The Wild Rice Harvesters

S INCE time immemorial, the Ojibwa people have
been the traditional rice harvesters of the
Great Lakes. September after September, in "the
Moon when the Rice is Harvested," whole clans of
them, Beavers and Herons, Loons and Foxes, paddled and portaged their way from all points of the
compass to converge on the shallow marshy lakes
fringed by the tall waving rice that would be a
staple insurance against the long cold winter ahead.
It was the highlight of the year; a time of reunion
after the summer's fishing, of festivities after the
day's work, and an opportunity for the young men
and maidens to meet, for they might not marry

within their own totem clan, with whom they would have spent the year.

The harvest moon still brings them here year after year to the same campsites on the shores of Whitefish Lake — digging on almost any point one can find arrowheads or shards of woodland Indian pottery — but nowadays the canoes are lashed to the tops of cars or trucks, and there are no more totem clans, only families. The older people still speak only Ojibwa, but almost all the younger generation are bilingual. They still beat the rice heads into the canoe by hand, but most of the grain is processed thereafter by machinery in Winnipeg, for every year there are fewer of the older generation willing and patient enough to process it in the traditional but time-consuming way, parching, husking and winnowing by hand — much to the regret of the connoisseur, for there is nothing to compare with the delicate smoky flavour of the local rice, the *mahnomonee* of the Ojibwa, the supreme complement to a wild duck dinner. And nowadays, with the machine processed product selling at about eight dollars a pound, a delicacy in the same category as caviar.

By the time that the wildfowling season has started, the Indians' canoes will be gone, leaving only beaten-down rice beds and reeds for the hunters' cover. Sometimes, in my first years in Canada, I was invited to shoot at Whitefish, which lies some

fifty miles west of Fort William in the Quetico region. Walking the far shore because I was too cold
to sit any longer in canoe or blind, I would come
across the deserted camping sites, and see the sap-
ling frames for tents or still-standing conical birchbark shelters, the blackened marks of the firesites.
Occasionally I found the birchbark platters used
for winnowing — my cat sleeps to this day in one of
these — or baskets, and marvelled at the ingenuity
and simplicity of their making, the spruce root sew-
ing that so adequately held them together. Although
I was not able to meet our local harvesters in person,
I found out about the harvesting and the history of
the Woodland Indians, and what I did not know
about them I supplied in imagination. Wandering
around the empty site with a gun, I would recreate
the activities and the people. "Here would be the
Rougeault's tents," I would tell myself, "and there
the Wahinegun's, and that one by itself must be Old
Grandma YesNo's. This was the pit where some
Luke, Job or Buck Deer trod the grain in long soft
moccasins to loosen the husks, and here . . ."

Then one year they came to life. Our respective
children re-interred in school, Susan and I had
stolen time to go up to the cabin at Whitefish before
the start of the hunting season, to fish, paint, and
laze instead. The harvesters were there to my excitement, for we could see smoke spiralling up through

the trees across the lake, but the canoes were far away at the head of the lake. We were fishing off a point across the lake, near the encampment, hoping to see them on the way back, when suddenly we heard women's voices singing. The cadences sounded sad and plaintive to our ears, but tonal interpretation must differ in Ojib for every now and then we heard giggling and soft laughter. It seemed a propitious time to try and buy some rice for supper. We beached the canoe and walked up a trail in the bush to the camp, our appearance effectively silencing the song. There were three old women sitting around a fire, all dressed in grubby black, the grandmothers, no doubt, left in camp to look after a horde of unkempt wildhaired children, two of whom I remember were playing a kind of complicated cat's cradle with string. I would have loved to find out about it — and about the odorous bearskin stretched on a frame. But the old women were uneasy and shy and could speak no English; they were obviously unhappy at the sight of Susan's sketchbook and, after a somewhat forced smile of admiration for the eczematous baby propped against a tree, the embroidered cloth of the cradle-board ragged and dirty, we left without the rice we had hoped to buy. That short encounter convinced me that it was better to stick to my imaginary inhabitants for the littered camp, as the present ones were far from savoury, and I was depressed at the only too evident poverty.

Some years passed during which there was no further meeting for disillusionment, although in that time I had come to know more of the reality of some Indians, mostly through those encountered on hunting trips on one hand, and those Ojibwa or Cree patients whom I had taught at the mental hospital — wildly differing examples, but at least they had cleared the romantic dreams out of my head, leaving a more practical and sympathetic understanding of the problems of twentieth-century Indians.

Then Susan and I once again drove up to White-fish, this time to hunt mushrooms, before the opening of the duck season. Our packsacks weighted down with food and great tomes on mycology, we hacked our way down the overgrown trail to the shack, followed by my long-suffering dog in this weekend's role of scarebear. On the narrow shore between the shack and the lake we looked out over the yellow heads of the bulrushes and past the thin green reeds of rice extending out for fifty yards or so to meet the blue rippled water. A mile across the water the hills in all the glory of their changing colour rose steeply, cloud shadows racing over them. There were redstarts among the rushes and secretive little marsh wrens, waxwings quarrelling cheerfully over the scarlet mountain-ash berries; and yellow birch leaves drifted singly across a brilliant blue sky. In the contrast after life in the city, even after the noise of the car's engine, colour was etched at its most vivid depth on one's first impression, and the peaceful silence fell as profoundly — only the lap of water against the reed bed, the waxwings, and far away the ringing of an axe.

Then, as we sat in the sun, drinking it all in, a flock of whistlers rose suddenly from the reeds, and through the rice beds before us, paddled slowly and effortlessly by the Indian in the bow, came a red canoe. Hunched in the stern a woman bent the long rice stems into the belly of the canoe with one short stick, knocking the husks off with another, all in one easy fluid motion. Slowly, silently, as though in a dream, they paddled out of sight beyond the bulrushes. Now, standing on the high bank to follow their progress, we could see out over the bed, and there, dotted all round the shores of the lake, we saw other canoes. We had timed it perfectly. The mushrooms were burgeoning, the harvesters were here, we could perhaps manage to get some rice this time; and besides, we had other reasons for visiting the camp if possible. Susan wanted to make sketches for a painting, and I wanted to rubberneck unobtrusively, for I had had the idea for a book set in this area simmering at the back of my mind for a long time. The only trouble was that we were both rather shy of barging in and possibly silencing everyone again, but we decided to meet that hurdle when we came to it.

We mushroomed all afternoon, and every now and then as we wandered along the trails on the hillside we would glimpse the lake below and see the small dots that were canoes moving back and forth among the rice. Towards the middle of the afternoon, we watched them return to the distant plumes of smoke that marked the campsites on the far shore. When they had eaten, we knew they would cross the lake for the rice-weighing at the Lands and Forests station. We kept watch on a sun-warmed rock, eating blueberries and identifying specimens as we waited. Below us an osprey plummetted down to a fish, and once in the clearing some thirty feet below a cross fox picked his noiseless way across the rocks with a peculiar hesitating gait. Suddenly aware of us, he paused and looked up, framed in the blazing orange of a sumac, and we saw then that he had only one foreleg.

An hour before sunset we were rewarded — the first of the canoes was putting out from the far shore, and soon we were able to count nineteen of them fanned out on the still water, an almost record number. Far down on the gravelled road below we could hear the rattling of the agent's truck, so we left our peaceful lookout, walked back to the car and drove down to the point to join him.

The Ojibwa are a quiet people and waste few words. One by one the canoes were beached in the mellow evening sunlight, and the men heaved out the bulging sacks and carried them up the shore to the weighing machine hanging outside a shed. There was a timeless quality about everything. The agent, a burly Finn, adjusted the scales, watched closely by the Indians, wrote the figures in a book, and the sacks were heaved into his truck. Cigarettes would then be lit, thumbs stuck into belts, and all would lean against the shed, staring into space until the next weighing. They were slim men mostly, in jeans and brightly coloured shirts, the young bucks favouring high-heeled Western boots, and all walking with the unmistakable slightly pigeon-toed gait. The women had remained, silent and unmoving, in the canoes, with the exception of a tall, magnificently hawk-faced woman and a dumpy granny, but even they stood apart and silent, their backs to the men, gazing across the lake. Two or three of the canoes had teenage girls as stern paddles, in white bobby socks and light, gaily coloured dresses. Everyone looked prosperous and immaculate. An enchanting little boy of about four erupted from a newly beached canoe, and for the first time Mrs. Hawkface and Grandma Dumpy showed some emotion, their faces cracking into smiles as he ran over to them, both trying to pull up his socks at the same

time, and both clucking lovingly over a scratch on
his wrist. He had long black hair and an almost Ori-
ental cast of feature, and his clear flute-like voice
carried in the still air so that even the men now
turned to watch him, smiling. But whenever he
came within earshot of us his brash older brother, a
high-school teenage type in horn-rimmed glasses
and knifepoint shoes, would answer him only in
slangy English; and when the little boy came up to
stroke and admire the horse mascot on my car,
"Steal it," said Brash One. "You're an Indian, aren't
you?" — cocking an eye for our reaction. But,
"Humph, humph, awoosh!" or something like that,
said Mrs. Hawkface sharply, with an imperious jerk
of her thumb, at which the teenager trotted off
smartly to help the men lift the sacks.

Susan sketched the little boy there and then, and
the impassive lines of Mrs. Hawkface softened vis-
ibly as she looked at it. "You too?" asked Susan persuasively, pointing to her sketchbook, and the granite face furrowed almost coyly. "Kinessa," she told
us, beaming, pointing to herself, and we introduced
ourselves. "You come tomorrow," she said, pointing
across the lake. "You make my cat, too, eh?" and
her finger moved in the direction of her canoe.
There on the bow thwart sat an aloof and battle-
scarred ginger tom. "Fifteen," said Kinessa proudly,
with all the tenderness of a mother for her only

child. "You come tomorrow — buy rice, too," she added guilefully. We were delighted; from all our hopes had come a bona fide invitation, the prospect of some factual rice, and now, added to this, was an irresistible waterborne cat and an apparently eager and willing sitter for Susan.

We took the freight canoe over next morning, leaving the dog behind to ensure harmonious relations with the cat, and from far out we could still hear his doleful wails of protest. Kinessa came down to the shore to meet us, and as she led the way up the trail to the camp she suddenly raised her voice and called out some order. We caught a brief glimpse of a woman scurrying into the bush carrying something. She reappeared almost immediately and plunged her arms back into a tub of washing on the ground before her tent. I longed, of course, to know the secret — hooch? Illicit game? Some pagan cult evidence or the rice agent's scalp?

Kinessa lost no time in falling into a pose, the pampered cat clasped to her laundered bosom, and I sat on a log and looked around in wonderment while Susan sketched. Gone were the grubby grannies and the dirty children. A long line of flannelette sheets had come out of the furtive one's washtub and hung in an incongruous backdrop against the trees at the other end of the clearing, and several small, plump, clean children gathered silently to watch Susan. A teenage girl lounged outside a tent — we learned later that she was Kinessa's almost blind great-grandchild — putting pincurls in her hair and listening to the Hit Parade on a transistor. Gone too were the raggedy stained canvas and birchbark shelters. Instead there were good solid large tents. Kinessa's was particularly imposing; there were fresh cedar boughs on the floor, a comfortable camp-bed with an immaculate bed-roll, and a tidy pile of quilts and blankets. Pinned to a mirror above a soapbox dressing table was a garish religious picture. The only thing that looked familiar from the last time I had seen this clearing peopled was the scraped skin of a large she-bear on a frame, its claws hanging in a small bag from a nearby tree. Later, I walked further along the trail and talked to an Indian with an even more surprising tent. Inside, it looked like an Abercrombie & Fitch advertisement for the Outdoor Life, from air mattress and incandescent lamp to all sorts of shiny cooking gadgets. He was a solitary man, which is unusual for an Indian, quiet spoken and most likable, who had served overseas for three years during the war. This probably accounted for the almost barrack-room neatness of his tent. He had gone back to the nomadic life by choice, spending his summers camping and fishing wherever he felt inclined. Then came the rice harvesting, and after that he would "get himself to

Banff," for he had always wanted to see the Rockies, until the winter trapping started. Rice? He always bought his, he said, smiling, the other was a little too crude for his taste.

Exploring further, I was relieved to find an authentic tub of rice parching on a slow fire. The washtub was suspended from an intricate arrangement of inter-relating branches forming a tripod, and was stirred every now and then by one of the women with a paddle. After this, Kinessa explained, showing us around, the parched grain went into a half barrel set in the ground to be pounded and stirred until the husks were free. This operation was presided over by an ancient man with an eleven-hair goatee beard who looked us over with rheumy reptilian eyes, then, clearly not liking what he saw, shifted the wad of snuff in his lower lip and spat dismissively into the fire. Kinessa spoke to him, but he turned his back on us with such a deafening silence, that she felt beholden to give us a mollifying demonstration of winnowing, skillfully pouring a handful of the barrel's contents from one shallow platter to another, until only the grain remained in one. Grandpa got up and hobbled obtrusively away. She produced an enamel cup and ladled out several pounds of the finished rice from the sack — dark-brown, long, slender grains with a delicious smoky aroma.

And when the harvesting was over, we asked on our way down to the canoe, Kinessa carrying her cat and a deep birchbark bag in which was her purse and a large alarm clock, "What then?" Back to her village in the Rainy River area, she told us, her husband was a guide at one of the hunting lodges near the border. In the summer she went with him to cook and fish and help portage the canoes when he guided at Quetico; but in the winter she was too busy to go as cook anywhere, for she was president of both the Parent-Teachers' Association, and the Ladies' Auxiliary of the Mission Guild. And it was in the winter, too, that she made the moccasins to sell to the summer tourist trade. Her great-granddaughter was waiting for her in the canoe. Kinessa took out her alarm clock and glanced at the time, settled the cat, pushed off and stepped into the canoe in one nimble action, then headed down the lakeshore. A red canoe emerged from further down and followed, the little boy we had seen the day before up in the bow with a slingshot, his father paddling. We could hear high, clear laughing as the canoe caught up, then Kinessa laughing too; less nimble, we pushed our own canoe out and headed back across the lake, our shameful engine shattering the peaceful lake until it was fouled into silence by the long rubbery stems of the water-lily pads.

We spent the rest of the afternoon in further

search of facts — grubbing around in a potato
patch further along the shore, finding two arrowheads and several shards of pottery along with the
rounded points used for pattern indentation. After
that, tireless as anyone in full tilt after a new interest, we climbed to the top of the high rocky bluff at
the far end of the lake in search of the rock en-
gravings that the owner of the potato patch had told
us were there — pictographs. But although we
searched diligently among the cones from the huge
white pines growing out from the very rocks themselves, turning back yards of orange lichen, we
found nothing but misleading natural indentations
in the smooth rounded rocks. At least there was a
reward in the glorious September view of the cloud-
shadowed lake framed in the turning trees, the great
sheer drop of cliff at the head glowing pink in the
sun. (And there *were* pictographs up there for next
time, we heard later — two lots, in fact, of the
strange enduring rock paintings . . .)

"How much did you pay old Kinessa?" asked the
agent later. "A quarter more than I paid, and
weighed on the scales!" he said smugly when we
told him. "And I'll bet she told you that mug of hers
holds a pound of rice?"

"Yes," we admitted, humbly but cheerfully, for
we felt that all in all Kinessa had given us good
measure that day.

3

Lake Nipigon

KINESSA had given us more than good measure, although Susan and I did not know then that we were starting off on years of a most satisfying collaborative interest in the Indian people that was to lead us into many and varied settlements, and cause us to read deeply — and with meaningful application to the people we met and the places we visited — of the history and cultural background of the Ojibwa. From that one encounter there had been revealed such an abysmal ignorance; now there was so much that we wanted to know, even the smallest things; why did Grandpa have such an obvious dislike of us? Because we were white, or because we were women? Was the laughter from the canoes directed at us? And where on earth were they going that day anyway, with a slingshot and an alarm clock? Why was time — so unusually — of the apparent essence? What did these people do when the white man was not around — what did they think? What was the purpose of the bear's claws, and what secret was hidden in the little skin drawstring bag around the little boy's neck? And how very very maddening it was not to understand, or be able to speak, one word of their language . . . And the pictographs, the artifacts — when, how, where? The list was endless.

Some of the answers were supplied that summer when we were fortunate enough to become involved in the uncovering of a vast archaeological workshop site, dating back thousands of years and containing much of the tool and weapon making history of Kinessa's Aquo-Plano ancestors. This drove our interest even deeper — in hopes of finding other sites, and further, for it seemed that each new fascinating piece of information led to the opening up of more and more tantalising paths to be explored — in short, we were hooked.

The following spring on a bitter day in May, we went up to stay on our first reserve, on the shores of Lake Nipigon. In the last sixty miles the road was pure sand and treacherous with spring washouts, later deteriorating into boneshaking boulders. On the way we met one other car coming in the opposite direction, the schoolteacher's, in whose schoolhouse we were going to stay, off for a short vacation in the city. He explained some of the more intimate problems of the propane gas stove and refrigerator; warned us not to leave anything lying around, not to allow any Indians across the threshold, and to be sure to lock all doors and windows. Finally he wished us well in a hopeless sort of way, and we lurched and bumped on, wondering if we were as mad as he seemed to think we were. Even the land we were passing through now seemed to grow more sombre by the moment, for we were entering the ravaged area of a bush fire that had swept across thousands of acres, levelling the timber to stark blackened stumps.

The schoolteacher's dire outlook was not news to us, for this particular reserve had quite a notorious reputation — wild goings-on, the occasional body left after a week-long drinking session, etc., and always it had been the same old story from anyone who had any dealings with the people: they were "dishonest," "completely degraded by drink," "totally unreliable," (I am quoting from a notebook of verbatim remarks); and furthermore, self-destructive, for if any among them attempted to climb out of the general slough of despond and put through some improvement, publicly beneficial, he might have his following, but invariably there would be an obstructive percentage; the factions would then split with a vengeance, one side ganging up on the other, producing many bloody heads and the eventual appearance of a long procession in the magistrate's court.

But we wanted to find out for ourselves: the nomadic harvesters were one aspect of local Indian life, a traditional one; whereas if these people had a tradition it was one of an association with alcohol dating back at least two hundred years: "Just how demoralising the rum was was indicated by the following excerpts from the journal of a fur trader in 1778: '. . . with the rum we gave them they continued in a state of inebriety three days and nights, during which frolic they killed four of their own party.' In another instance, 'I traded for their skins and furs and gave them some rum, with which they had a frolic which lasted for three days and nights; on this occasion five men were killed, and one woman dreadfully burned. . . .' " *

For any group to survive after two hundred years of such decimating frolics would seem to indicate a Darwinian hardiness and resistance. We had open minds on the whole issue — principally because we had no knowledge or experience with which to fill

* George I. Quimby, *Indian Life in the Upper Great Lakes: 11,000 B.C. to A.D. 1800*, 2 vols. (University of Chicago Press, 1960).

the open space. However, I remember that in our innocence and gullibility we had brought a shotgun along — expecting perhaps a hooch-crazed mob of the degraded, unreliable, dishonest and factious populace to break into the schoolhouse? (Had we known it then, if they had come looking for firewater they would have been disappointed: we ourselves found only a bottle labelled "Holy Water" in the icebox.)

The first evening there did seem rather gloomy and foreboding — from the howling dogs to the dark faces pressed against dirty windowpanes illuminated from within by candles or the yellow light of lamps as we unloaded the car in the dusk. But I think my deepest impression was of cars: cars everywhere, in every yard one at least, abandoned, rusty and sagging, as horrible an eyesore as only derelict cars can be; and those that still had some unmuffled life in them being driven up and down, up and down the one street by long-haired youths. We shut the door of the schoolroom behind us, conscientiously locking and bolting it, very conscious of the unseen silent watchers, but feeling more self-conscious than anything else. If there was any frolicking that night we heard nothing of it, only the sounds of a guitar and some people singing and laughing for a while. Even the noise of the cars died away soon, leaving only the howling. Every now and then there would be a volley of what we took to be Ojibwa oaths, followed by the yelp of a dog, then silence again. (They were probably all stoning themselves in the town, and spent the night in a ditch, said the Hudson's Bay clerk contemptuously next day, who loathed this place and could not wait to be transferred. He was, as are so many of the Bay personnel, a Scot.)

After supper, looking around for something to read, I picked up an R.C. missal lying on the bookcase, and belonging to the teacher. It was printed in Scotland "under the auspices of the Diocese of Glasgow," and there I read with much interest prayers for "the appalling evil of mixed marriages," religiously mixed, of course; and then, somewhat to my indignation, for "the *conversion* of Scotland." It was quite a shock — Susan and I had not realised before that we were so categorically beyond the spiritual pale (one the product of "appalling evil," and the other an environmental heretic) that people of our own *race* had to pray for us. How far — or how narrowly — could bigotry extend? And what *presumption*. . . . For the first time I had a glimpse of how it must feel to be a happy innocent heathen and suddenly wake up one day to find an influx of strangers in your midst, impertinently praying over you, and doing their dedicated best to convert you to another way of life, a life having no bearing whatsoever, either spiritually or physically, on the life you were leading, so that from the moment you embarked upon it you would be completely lost and at sea. . . . No wonder that ecologically happy heathen, the Ojibwa Indian, went under when he took on the gods of the white people. Particularly on top of the rum. "It was these Indians, deprived of their aboriginal culture and left in a badly depressed economic situation, who made the last futile but bloody attempts to delay white settlement of the Upper Great Lakes region. A cultural continuity that had lasted about 13,000 years was destroyed by the advance of Old World civilisation." These were the last lines in the next book I picked up, one I had brought with me.*

Later, about nine o'clock, there was a knocking at the schoolroom door beyond the sitting room ("Eeny meeney miney mo — *you* go," I said to Susan, mindful of the teacher's warning; "And ira dira dominu — out goes *you*," said Susan firmly. We both went.) The flashlight revealed a short, thickset man, his face dark and deeply pock-marked under his peaked cap, and wearing a parka, torn and stained in contrast to the beautiful shining wolf fur round the hood now lying on his shoulders. He shut the blade of a knife lying in his hand, then introduced himself as Steve Wapageesik: one of us must

* Quimby, *Indian Life in the Upper Great Lakes.*

have dropped this on the way in, he said, and handed my pocket knife over. If there was any trouble with the furnace let him know — he lived in the second house down. Or if there was anything else we wanted to know? The schoolteacher vanished in a puff of smoke as we asked Mr. Wapageesik in to have some coffee, and as he took his boots off to do so I nipped ahead and shoved the embarrassing gun under the sofa.

Sitting on it with his coffee, carefully dropping his cigarette ash into the palm of his hand until we provided a saucer, it was quite obvious that he wanted to know, in a roundabout way, why we were there, who had sent us — and that his visit was primarily an excuse for this. We made it very clear that we were there for no other reason than that we *wanted* to be there — to paint, and to fish. Susan got out some sketches of the rice gatherers, and he was fascinated, wanting to know all about them. Could he round up some children as sitters for her tomorrow, she wanted to know? Could he tell me where to go fishing?

Disarmed by such innocent pastimes, relieved undoubtedly that we did not represent officialdom in any way, he left, promising everything that we asked.

"Never leave anything lying around," had already been discounted; how about "totally unreliable" for tomorrow, we wondered, and retired to our sleeping bags, wakened intermittently by the howling of the dogs drifting through the window which should have been shut and locked but wasn't.

Next morning, almost before we had finished breakfast, there was a group of small runny-nosed volunteers outside the schoolroom, and even some adults. Susan set up a studio among the desks and got to work, and with four or five little boys as guides I went off to fish below the rapids above the bridge. It was bitterly cold, and, casting from a rock with flurries of snow blowing in my face, I was glad of a parka, yet none of my guides wore more — outwardly anyway — than a shirt and denim jacket, and one of them was barefoot. They sniffed steadily on the bank behind me, seldom speaking unless I asked them a question. I persuaded them to give me a lesson in elementary Ojibwa, and they were painstaking about my pronunciation, although obviously hard put to contain their mirth over some of the results; but it was only when I laughed myself that they joined in openly. Did they like school? Shrug and blank faces. Weren't they cold? This question seemed to surprise them. One of them volunteered that one day last winter it had been 60° below zero — too cold even for school. The family had stayed in bed to keep warm. They all had a turn with the fishing rod, but we only caught two pick-

erel and two pike. Where would they go when they
had finished grade school here? Go? They would
stay here. Wouldn't they go on to high school? The
idea of this convulsed them; high school would
mean the Indian residential school, or, as a last re-
sort, being farmed out as a boarder in town — the
idea was too horrible to contemplate apparently. I
asked them about the great bush fire of five years
before. Although they could not have been more
than four or five at the time, they remembered vividly — it had been the event of their lives. They had
been evacuated to an island on the lake along with
the women and old people. All the able men in the
area had been out fighting the fire. What the children most vividly remembered from their ringside
view was the red sky lighting up the land for miles
around at night, the smell, and the ash-laden wind
that had reached them even on the island.

I asked the biggest if he could clean the fish with
my knife, but he shook his round black head, and
the blank look that was to become so familiar to me
in the future settled on his face. They could have the
rest of the fish if they would just clean one for me, I
suggested persuasively. Finally he said that we
could take them back and he would tell one of his
sisters, or his mother, to clean them. I wondered if I
had asked him to do something below masculine

dignity — perhaps cleaning fish was purely a woman's job? I asked, but they just looked covertly at one another, so we left it at that.

His mother was a vast shapeless figure held together with safety pins, her long hair tied back from her face with a bootlace, and one eye half closed and swollen, a real sunset of a black eye. Despite this, she had a slow pleasant smile. Behind her skirts as she stood in the doorway small dirty faces peered out at varying heights, but as they kept appearing and disappearing I had no idea whether there were three or thirty, politically deciding to admire them all anyway — rather wasting my words as they turned out to be neighbours' children. She asked me to come in, but I saw as she shifted her weight that the room was crowded with people and suddenly I panicked (finding it hard enough to meet a sudden strange mass of my own race most of the time) and gave the excuse that I had to get back to the schoolhouse to eat, but said that I would come back for the fish later. Halfway over the street I realised what a coward I was being. If I didn't get over this idiotic shyness here and now there wouldn't be much hope for future relationships with Indian people. Whereupon I turned back and asked if I could come in and for once learn how to clean a fish properly. ("You can't get to first base with those crazy whites," I imagined them saying to one another afterwards.

"They'll say one thing and do another the whole time. . . .")

So in I went, removing my rubber boots on the top step. My sock came off with the first one, something that I would not normally bother to report, but — "Toenails!!!!" says my notebook of that day — "??? Religious significance; tribal markings; gangrene???" A week before, for some passing whim, (perhaps as a protest against the weather) I had painted my toenails bright green. Now, for one brief second before I got my sock back on again, here they were exposed — and in just about the last place I would have chosen. My hostess's open beady eye had lit on them, and although there was no expression on her face I wondered how she was accounting for them, what they *meant*. I mention this at some length now, for it was something that was to come back to me time and time again in the years ahead. If I learned one thing that day at Lake Nipigon, it was nothing to do with moral issues of overcoming cowardice, but to take things for their face value. If the boot had been on the other foot, the toenails on some Indian foot, my busy little mind would have been searching for some significance — green toes for some spring fertility rite? An ancient cult? To keep the Windigos away? Never again did I see something bizarre without thinking, well, perhaps it's just another Green Toenail . . .

After my head cleared — the atmosphere was stifling, particularly after the cold outside — the roomful of people resolved into six adults and four children. Nobody seemed to be doing anything but sitting, one very old woman and two middle-aged ones on the bed, three younger ones on a bench. There was nothing else to sit on, and the rest of the furniture consisted of a table (a piece of board across two oil drums) and a wood stove. Various bundles hung from nails, or were stowed in corners. There were some tins on an open shelf, and a kerosene lamp, two pots and a kettle by the stove, and that was all. I knew that the little boy's name was Joe Wetereesik, and after smiling blurrily around introduced myself and called his mother Mrs. Wetereesik, but she turned out to be Mrs. Mackwa while still the boy's mother. I tried to link up the children, who by now had all climbed onto the bed and sat on a pile of blankets and clothes regarding me as silently as everyone else. A small naked one seemed to have a rash over most of his body and was scratching his head suspiciously. I admired them all again and learned their names. They belonged to the youngest woman, so for want of something to do I pulled out pictures of my own children from my wallet and showed them to her. These were passed around, along with some cigarettes which seemed to break the ice. The fact that I had nothing but daughters brought about an almost cosy all-girls-together atmosphere, with everyone apparently sympathetic about my sonless, consequently low-status, state. In the meantime, Mrs. Mackwa pushed back a pan of scummy water, some socks, half a loaf of bread, and a few half-empty tins on the table, rummaged around until she found a knife (under the bed) and swiftly gutted and filletted the fish. Then, sweeping off the remains with one hand into another, she opened the door and cast it forth where it was instantly gobbled up by a dog who seemed to materialize from nowhere almost before the fish-guts hit the ground. I could hardly keep my eyes off the ancient woman who smoked as though she was entirely hollow. No matter how deeply she dragged on the cigarette, no smoke ever again appeared.

I asked if I could try my hand at another fish, and my amateurish efforts with the knife, after Mrs. Mackwa's professional attack, produced smiles and giggling. Nobody looked like a silent Gorgon any more. I relaxed and began to enjoy myself. The hurdle was over . . .

I left soon after, and, comparing notes with Susan, found that she too had been visiting, and that we had had much the same feelings. The fact that she has three sons did not give her my cosily superior Poor Woman rapport with the women, but pencil and paper were great icebreakers — and reassur-

ingly familiar in an unfamiliar world and the long silences of a language and custom barrier. She had had a wonderful morning in the schoolhouse, putting things on a business basis which she kept to from there on — paying a quarter to children to sit, and fifty cents to a dollar for adults, and had found the children biddable and most cooperative.

It is a truism that the first time is always the hardest. Never again were we to feel the awkwardness and uncertainty of those days. We found that silence need not be socially awkward, but relaxing and pleasant. The only thing that mattered really was that one truly liked the people, and as *people* — not as examples of this, that or the other, or as potential material for facts or information. The other fortunate thing for future relationships was that neither of us had very much reverence for the normal white household gods, so that much that would have appalled others in terms of obvious disorder or squalor either passed blissfully over our heads, or else we became so used to it that we never noticed — like the Indians themselves, in fact. Cigarettes or candies are icebreakers everywhere in the world. I was to find photographs a great help as well — particularly those that I had taken in other reserves. Perhaps most important of all we learned to let other people's unconstructive opinions flow gently by into oblivion.

On Sunday morning we heard another screaming of brakes, but this time it was the Roman Catholic Father who had come to take the morning service in the little wooden church at the end of the village street. He was accompanied by a young seminarian who sat in the tiny gallery with a tall woman whom we had noticed in the village because she seemed to be dressed a cut above everyone else and was actually wheeling a baby carriage, and together they sang the responses. I recognised one of the sacristans, now cherubic in white lace and scarlet cassock, as being one of my fishing guides; the other sacristan was about to come down with measles — he had confided to Susan minutes before the service that he felt "awful sick" and we wondered whether he would stay the course as his face grew gradually as red as his cassock and his eyes more glazed. After the service the Father and the seminarian girded up their robes and charged on to the baseball field adjoining the church. Both knew every last child by name and spoke fluent Ojibwa, and both seemed to be enjoying themselves as much as the youngsters.

Reading my description of him now is as though I were reading a generic description of all the missionary fathers I was later to meet: "Essentially open-minded, and dedicated to Indian mission for 25 years; the people come first, the religion second. Eyes open to all faults, but lovingly — feels education is the only cure-all for these people: education, *education*, EDUCATION!!! Has seen it work time and time again with youngsters sent to St. Joseph's to board, away from home environment; and always the deterioration when they return. Isn't it bad to break family ties? Aren't they terribly homesick, bewildered? Of course it's bad, in a normal society, he says, but for this generation we will have to be cruel to be kind if there's to be any hope for the next generation. . . ."

I further note that he and the seminarian came for dinner that night, and that we gave them "curry, chicken, mushrooms, steak, pickerel — all together!" We must have been finishing up the leftovers in the refrigerator. However, apparently they survived this gastronomic nightmare, for my next entry is of a morning's fishing with the Father, when between snow flurries the sky would suddenly clear, and the birds around burst into optimistic song once more.

How deep was poverty here, I wanted to know of him, thinking of the bare houses, the ragged clothes, yet knowing that these did not necessarily have an intrinsic bearing; what truth in the stories of Skid Row degradation here, we ourselves having found the people polite and pleasant, and the children who hung around the schoolhouse better behaved than a comparable group of white children — we had missed nothing, although we had left plenty lying around. Was it true that "today no one starves but many are frequently hungry?"

Yes, he said, poverty went very deep, but drink was the devil here; together they created a vicious cycle, for the means to alleviate one was also the means to alleviate, for the moment, having to think about it. The trapping had been meagre since the fire devastation, and there had been years of poor fishing. The population had expanded beyond these resources long before. Children brought the government baby bonus — but for the rest there was only Welfare Relief when the Lands and Forests spring re-forestation work was over, until the fall, when in the falsest of false economies the men were paid ten dollars a day for planting trees on their own reserve land. They never thought beyond the day, which was hardly surprising, and when they received the tree-planting or welfare cheque it was only too natural for a group of them to hire a taxi for sixty dollars and drive the eighty miles into the town's beer parlours and taverns (liquor not being allowed on the reserve), and there forget tomorrow and the waking up to their ordained place on the very bottom rung of democracy's ladder; there, too often meeting only the white Skid-Row equivalent, and seldom the decent average Joe — certainly never would they see inside the latter's home to gain even an inkling of

how he lived. They were like children who spend all
their allowance the first day in the candy store. As
children they must be as patiently taught; and as
children must grow up and get out in the world and
fend for themselves, so must they.

If people thought conditions were bad here, he
added, they should go forty miles along the shore
where another band who had left their reserve to
take up a gypsy life after the last war were presently
squatting in tents or one-room shacks in almost in-
describable squalor, the children never going to
school or receiving medical attention for it was impossible to locate them long enough.

He told us, as so many others who loved and were
concerned about the Indians, that, before it was too
late and the outside world irrevocably caught up
with them, we should get to know the people of the
far northern bands. The rice gatherers had been an
example of a successful adjustment between both
the old and the new world. Lake Nipigon was a
good example of what happens to the Indian who
lives too close to, yet never is a part of, white so-
called civilisation. The northern people in places
like Pikangikum, Big Trout or Sandy Lake were
something else altogether.

Early in the morning the day we left, I watched
the men going off to the tree-planting in a bus, some
of them riding on the top. They were an unsmiling

lot, with none of the badinage one would expect for the latecomers who leaped onto the roof. There was nothing of the "heigh-ho, heigh-ho, it's off to work we go" — if anything, they looked as though they were being transported to the salt mines. ("Probably all got hangovers," snarled the Hudson's Bay Clerk.) Maria, the woman who had sung in church, went by with her clean baby in its status baby carriage — alone, as always. Maria had a rough row to hoe, apparently, in her efforts to pull herself and her family up the social scale. The women laughed at her openly and said she was giving herself white airs. She owned a lawn mower for her pocket-sized square of grass, and it stood by her tidy woodpile with a "for rent" sign hanging from the handle. But no one ever rented it; no one wanted a lawn or a tidy yard, and sometimes to show what they thought of such ostentatious foolishness the women would throw rubbish on the little green patch. At night, of course. Some of the little boys who had gone fishing with me were there too. School started tomorrow, they informed me sorrowfully, looking like small editions of their fathers.

Looking at them that morning, with their bad teeth, their runny noses and skinny little frames, I wondered what on earth the future did have in store for them, with their ambition to stay here. At what age would they learn to drink their miseries away, eke out an existence by an inadequate trapline with a Relief cheque, chop down the trees their fathers had planted so that they could plant more, marry and have children — many children; plant, chop, children, drink?

The houses these children came from, I knew, had been erected ten years ago by the Department of Indian Affairs to replace the former shacks and tents. A step forward undoubtedly, but why did everything have to halt after providing four walls and a roof? "Ten years is a long time; long enough to adjust to weatherproof windows and walls for even the most primitive people on earth; long enough, therefore, for running water, drains and electricity to have followed naturally. Why do we always have to hold something back when we give? What good is half-baked magnanimity? So what if they chop up the floors, plug the drains or fuse the lights at first? It's the same, stupid, long-ago discounted talk that one used to hear about the Glasgow slums — 'give them a decent place to live in and they'll put the coal in the bath,' etc., etc. Instead of paying them to plant on their own land, why not pay them for the installation of drains and water and a generator?"

I am quoting from the notebook I kept at the time; idealistic; unaware then of any other issue than that which immediately confronted me; ignorant of the workings, economical or otherwise, of Indian Affairs; unaware of white indifference to the whole subject, or the Indian's apathy about his own condition. There was much to learn.

This was a sad place. It still is. It will be a long time before they frolic, in the more accepted sense of the word, at the present rate of progress.

4

The People of the Big Trout Band

THE SEVENTEENTH-CENTURY fur traders who first explored inland from Hudson Bay paddled upstream on the mighty Severn River, threading a desolate route through the treeless tundra, muskeg and swamp, until at last, endless portages after, they came to the stunted pines and great expanse of water that was to become known as Big Trout Lake. Here they found the nomadic bands of the Ojibwa people friendly and helpful, their country rich in fur-bearing animals. Thereafter, they returned at infrequent intervals to barter for the pelts the Ojibwa had trapped, but for nearly two hundred years these traders, Highland Scots for the main part, were the only white people to penetrate this

wilderness, and the way of life of its people remained virtually unchanged, except that some of the
children now bore strange names like Roderick
Cromarty or Kirsty McKay.

Susan and I flew there from Sioux Lookout, the
last little town from where most of the bush planes
take off for the Arctic watershed areas between
Lake Superior and Hudson Bay. It was a three-hour
journey, but we were crammed into the Beechcraft
like any voyageur into his canoe, amongst our own
gear, canvases and easel, dufflebags, sleeping bags
and typewriter, fishing rod and geologists' picks,
along with a sack of onions, bales of wire, and
heaven knows what else. Just as we were wondering
how we could endure it for three hours, a large Indian carrying an axe appeared and was somehow
crammed in too. Gently, effortlessly, he allowed
himself to be absorbed into a bed of onions and wire,
laid his head on a box of nails, and fell asleep, occasionally waking to point out something of interest
with his axe-head, but, apart from the shaft of an
abandoned mine, and sometimes a straight slash
through the bush to a lake's edge that marked the
winter road of the toboggan-towing tractor-train,
there was little to see but the endless stretch of dark
land across which gleaming shapes of water, scattered or interlocking, lay like giant jigsaw pieces.
Sometimes I could trace the course of a winding

river and mark the white splashes of the rapids, or when we flew lower I watched ducks fly up from the lakes as our shadow passed over them, but in all that land I only once saw a trace of man; two canoes crossing a lake and, in a clearing, the outline of a tent — trappers or prospectors, probably.

We had chosen Big Trout for this very remoteness. It is the most northerly Ojibwa settlement in northwest Ontario, and its people therefore among the least affected by outside influence of their nation. The first missionary did not come until 1900, and he himself was an Indian, converted to the Anglican faith, who understood their ways. He made such an indelible impression on his people that today his faith predominates in numbers of congregations all over these northern settlements. But apart from the widely scattered posts of the Hudson's Bay Company that followed in the wake of the fur traders, it was not really until the advent of the small amphibious bush-plane that full contact with the white world was made. Long after the dignity of their cousins in the South had disintegrated under the influence of the white man they remained complete and whole in the life that their people had led since time unknown.

The Crown had made a treaty in 1905 under which the various scattered bands were combined into that of the official Big Trout Band, but continued to live on their "reserved" settlements. Officialdom had arrived, with health and welfare services, but was only seen once a year as it still had to make the long arduous journey by canoe or York boat from Hudson Bay.

Under the terms of the treaty, a family was awarded a square mile of their land, and annuities of $4.00 per head guaranteed, to be paid out at an annual Celebration. The area ceded by the Indians was 90,000 square miles. The down-payment for this sizeable chunk of land — or Treaty Presents as the Crown preferred to call them — was $8.00 per head, and an unspecified "number of flags" (it would seem that other treaty recipients did much better with their presents from the strange coffers from which the Crown dug out these little extras, such as balls of twine, medals, ammunition, a sack of potatoes or assistance in case of pestilence). The Indians were allowed to hunt, trap and fish in the ceded area, subject to government regulations. The Crown maintained a firm hold even on the reserves — the right to restrict settlers, to sell land (subject to compensation), the right to act as lessees. The government paper, from which I quote, explaining the difference in treaties made with groups like the Iroquois who emigrated to Canada from what is now the United States and were given reserve land, and treaties made with the original inhabitants, such as

the "Ojibwa, Cree and Others of Northwest Ontario," describes the latter as "those whose aboriginal interest in the soil of Upper Canada had to be
extinguished." A curious way of putting it. One
wonders if the "unspecified number of flags" was
for the people to wave at the celebration of their extinction.

Nevertheless, celebrate they do, and that was why
we had come now, for the treaty pay-out would draw
the families in from the traplines and fishing camps
to the main settlement on Post Island, providing
plenty of subject material for Susan, who wanted to
paint them, and plenty of conversation for me to listen to. I had been trying to learn something of their
language for some time, but my grammar and
phrase book were of the "Lo, the postilion has been
struck by lightning" vintage, and I wanted to up-
date my vocabulary. Both Cree and Ojibwa are
polysyllabic languages, with a tricky, aspirated "h,"
and many subtle nuances of pronunciation, so that
there is many a pitfall between the written and oral
word. Treaty time would have the additional advan-
tage for me of having an interpreter on hand during
the pay-out.

We had been on other reserves, but had never
flown into one as remote as this, and everything was
of absorbing interest as we craned from the windows of the Beechcraft circling low over the settle-

ment on Post Island below; the neat squares of church and rectory, nursing station and Hudson's Bay post, the fenced-in compound of the weather station, all tidily together on the high part of the island, then, straggling down to the water's edge, a collection of log cabins and conical canvas matagwans. Soon we could make out the canoes drawn up on the shore, dogs staked nearby, then a line of scurrying ant-like figures heading along paths cut through muskeg and low Labrador tea to converge on the dock to which we were now taxiing.

We were to learn later that the pattern of arrival at all the other settlements we visited never varied. Always there was the watchful appraising semicircle at the end of the dock; the women and girls in one group, giggling into the backs of their hands, kerchiefed heads turned sideways in a gesture that we were to find in no way represented merriment or ridicule but simply a shy uncertainty on how else to behave; the children in front or peering from behind their mothers' skirts, some babies slung over shoulders in laced-up tikkanagans, the carrying boards, or propped upright against some handy support, all with their hands stuffed into mouths; the men, a close silent group, stuffed theirs into hip pockets. They unloaded us into the sudden cold and utter silence along with the onions, bales, and our own stock of gear — Susan's canvases, easel and paints

coming in for a good deal of interested comment. I
felt envious. All the world loves a painter. Their
magic is visual and above-board, fascinating to even
the smallest child. All they have to do is set up an
easel or start sketching — an audience materialises
immediately — and contact is made. Even as we
were walking up the dock, running the gamut of
those frankly staring eyes, I realised that I was going to have to find myself a profession as obvious as
Susan's if I wanted to be accepted by, and consequently listen to, these people. Nothing could be
more inhibitive to conversation than a silent white
woman making occasional furtive notes in a little
black book. Big White Sister is Listening to You
. . . for how was anyone to know that they were
simply new words and not a secret report on unsani-
tary garbage or truant school child? Unfortunately,
the only other occupations I had in mind involved
field glasses, camera, and a small pick for pottering
quests after birds, wild flowers and rocks. Slung
around with this equipment I would look even more
sinister.

We settled into the empty hut that Bert Cone, the
Free Trader, had very generously put at our dis-
posal. It had stored furs all winter, and was now
cosily furnished with two cots, a large and ravenous
wood stove, and half a lunch counter. It was spa-
cious and light, with many windows — rather too

many as we sometimes felt as exposed as fish in an aquarium to the interested eyes of the inhabitants — and by the time we scrounged a couple of apple boxes, Bert had hooked up a propane cooker, and his wife contributed some household equipment and blankets, we were in paradise. There was an out-house, scenically situated among the Labrador tea about fifty yards away, and a unique running water system: one stood at the door with a bucket and hailed the first passing Indian child who was only too delighted to run to the lake and fill it for a hand-ful of candies.

It was still very cold — the ice had only just broken up in the lake — and a bitter wind swept down from the north. I had hardly settled down by the wood stove on my apple box to thaw out than Susan had set up a studio in the corner and installed the first of a succession of picturesque but fre-quently unwashed models on hers. The temperature climbed as the wood stove reddened. The windows were sealed, an untanned bearskin in the corner made itself known; so did the model's pungently hand-tanned caribou moccasins. Friends, relatives and children dropped in to see if being a model was a painless process. If reassured, they would be per-suaded themselves. The bearskin, humanity, and moccasins by the dozen fought for supremacy. There was certainly plenty of opportunity for conversation, if one could remain conscious. I would have to give up the idea of using Susan as a lure for conversation and new friends if I wanted to survive for the next few weeks. . . . Ten minutes later I remembered the knitting I had stuffed into my case at the last minute, and, armed with my needles, I went forth, thankfully, to meet the populace in my new profession of Knitter (Extraordinary).

It worked like a charm. Wherever I went my sad sock accompanied me, already three years on the needles and looking every minute of it, a grubby yellow tube, growing longer and longer, as I only knew how to knit in one direction, until by the time I left Big Trout it looked like a turtle-neck collar for a giraffe. But, it worked. It disarmed and made friends and was a conversation piece. It was wonderful camouflage, for I could drop my eyes to it and give it my absorbed attention when I did not want people to think I was giving it to them. Or I would prop myself against a woodpile and be sure that sooner or later some small girls would arrive to try their hands at a row or two, which led of course to their teaching me new words or correcting my pronunciation with much giggling.

The cold persisted that first week — there was even snow — but the quietness remained, broken only by the outbursts of howling dogs at night, or the occasional aircraft engine, and I realised, after a while, that it was not just because we were hundreds of miles from any road or railway, but because the Indians are naturally a quiet, soft-spoken people, and all sound is muted by the paths cut through the muskeg. Rubber boots were standard footwear, of necessity, and all removed them before entering a house, like the Japanese their sandals, except that here they brought the boots inside, as anything left outside would have been torn to pieces by the packs of starving dogs roaming the island.

During the first two days there was a lot of activity around the settlement with families coming from distant traplines or moving back to their summer quarters at Big Trout. Tents sprang up beside cabins, and dogs, puppies and children were everywhere. The washing lines sagged with the weight of winter clothes, quilts and blankets. Over all, there was a general air of festivity, with a spanking trade done in new clothes and small luxuries on the proceeds of the winter's furs or tomorrow's treaty bonus. Everyone — but everyone — was there, unless they were in hospital or out fighting forest fires, for the very good reason that if they missed the annual X-raying that took place as well they might miss out on welfare cheques.

The treaty party, consisting of agent, assistant, and welfare officer, arrived in a Cessna, the X-ray Party with all their equipment in a Norseman, hard on their heels. The schoolroom was cleared for action, the flag run up. I made myself as small and invisible as possible, squeezed into a school desk in a corner where I could hear the interpreter and prepared to knit the day away as a spectator. Susan, perched on a desk at the back of the room, sketched throughout.

Not so very long ago, Treaty Day was a colourful dress-up occasion for everyone, with scarlet-coated Mounties, the gleam of silver dollars, and even sometimes the incongruous white of flannels in a cricket match afterwards. Nowadays the only people who still dress up at Big Trout are the Indians, the women in their most colourful skirts and kerchiefs — purple, red, and kelly green were popular this year — the little boys in stiff new jeans and pristine running shoes, the store creases still obvious in their T-shirts, and sometimes the price tag still on. The little girls looked angelic, with their black hair brushed to an unusual shininess, or neatly braided, sometimes in party dresses, white socks and shoes, all shining like peeled hazel nuts, but more often they wore the traditional adult-length skirts that make them look like quaint little women. Some of the older men even wore unaccustomed suits and ties for the occasion. Those who were wearing their best clothes insisted on the formality of shaking hands with the agent. I felt that they missed the bygone dignities of dress and ceremony. It seemed a pity that, as the people themselves dressed up for the occasion, the white people did not put on more of a show.

The Mounties are gone nowadays, their presence, one gathers, having rather dampened the gala air of the day and caused some absenteeism, being inevitably associated with the long arm of the law — and the silver dollars have turned to mundane cheques. The only note of government colour was the Union Jack covering the schoolmaster's desk at which the agent sat, flanked by the interpreter and the assistant, checking and verifying names and numbers of dependants in a large black ledger, while the people filed slowly past, receiving their cheque when they had been ticked off.

This was the general pattern of all the other outlying settlements which would be visited in turn, although some might hold a dance or Sports Day afterwards. At Big Trout there was one other presence to add a unique tone to the proceedings. This was Willy, whose personal uniqueness lay in the fact that he is not only racially Mongolian, being an Ojib, but he is also a mongoloid of classic textbook appearance, and limited intelligence, even to the sparse, thin hair (which seems particularly out of place on an Indian as they almost always have extremely thick hair) and the happy extroverted disposition that is so often found. He loved dressing up, and usually wore three or four ties flapping outside his several shirts or sweaters. One would see him popping in and out of tolerant doors in the village, gathering here a cigarette, there a bar of chocolate, shaking hands all round like a pump handle or snapping into a magnificent salute of Guards-like precision. This year he was really dressed for the occasion. Somewhere, someone — the agent, I suspect — had gathered together a remarkable uniform for him: Mountie hat and boots, breeches and jacket of 1914 vintage, and there were at least six chevrons painted on one arm along with the insignia of "Martins Light Horse Infantry." Willy was installed at a desk in a corner of the schoolroom where he remained all day as the constant stream of treaty recipients filed before the agent, writing busily in a notebook in faithful imitation (endless rows of 9's), checking and okaying blank slips of paper that were occasionally handed back to him to keep him happy. Sometimes he hurried things along if they seemed to be slowing up, with an imperious pointing of the hand to the next in line. Yet his presence in no way mocked or made farcical the proceedings. He was simply Willy, filling the traditional niche that someone had made for him on this day many years ago, part of the accustomed scene and accepted with the tolerant affection due a mascot.

The caribou bone-scraper that hangs on the wall above my desk was made by Willy, his crude attempt at fashioning the customary thin edge, the ends daubed strangely in bright blue paint, like a prayer stick. It was the only thing he had ever managed to make and his old, immensely stout mother was so pathetically excited that she had panted up to the rectory with it almost before the paint was dry so that it could be glorified with a price tag along with the carvings, beadwork and moccasins that the minister sold on a cooperative basis for the people. I doubled the asking price, and for fifty cents I probably own the only bone-scraper made by a thirty-five-year-old Mongolian mongol in the whole world.

The welfare officer was busy that morning sorting out the new crop of applications for baby bonuses, old age pensions, etc. Babies were obviously booming as a long-term investment, and the majority of families departed with nice fat dividends — $4.00 per capita interest. And, looking around at the round-cheeked children, three, four, or nine, ten to a family, realising that this room represented one microscopic part of the global population explosion, I became fully aware for the first time of the sobering and paradoxical fact that it is not man's inhumanity to man that will bring about disastrous consequences to the generations ahead, but man's humanity.

On Treaty Day, the sunny schoolroom was vibrant with slow-moving colour, and sounds were muted and low, faces dignified and solemn as the Queen's, whose portrait looked down from the wall behind the flag-covered desk. Next day, X-ray day, was quite different. The room was alive with sound, fearful small children giving tongue at the sight of the nurses who were associated with needles and nostrums; gigglings of girls and women, gabblings of gossip, and occasional laughter and repartee from the men. Now yesterday's colour had given place to statuesque groups in the white X-ray gowns of the women and adolescent girls, interspersed with the undershirts in varying shades of white of the men and boys and little girls. Willy was there of course, in the role of helper this time, lifting children on and off the chair on which they stood to bring their chests into line with the X-ray plate, beckoning and pointing, organizing the waiting groups, who played along with him, with all the peremptoriness and authority of a king for a day. Steadily through the din one could hear the monotonously repeated instructions of the technicians at the X-ray machine: "*Sk-watchin-kabuhin*" (stand still), "*Qui-nahban*" (take a breath), then "*Meeway*" (that's all), and so on, to the next one, so many times that I found myself repeating it in my sleep that night. Or, uninhibited Australian shouts from Lew, one of the

nurses: "*Mind* your mussinegan. *Have* you got your
mussinegan? *Don't* lose your mussinegan," the precious orange X-ray cards that she filled out and
which guarantee the cheque. Or, "into the giggle
room, girls, and put on your gowns!" Marg, the
other nurse, would shout to a group of stout impassive matrons filing through the door, and who
understood not a word of English but nodded agree-
ably anyway. Those who had offspring in tikkanagans leaned them against a desk, while offspring no
longer portable were dumped on the floor beside us
where they sat silent and wide-eyed and completely
still as their massive Mums disappeared into the
cloakrooms to emerge some minutes later, self-
conscious and giggling like schoolgirls, trans-
formed into a band of stout Aimee Semple McPher-
son-like Angels, and were frisked for lurking safety
pins by Marg. Everything was done with efficiency
and speed, for the entire population, about four hundred and fifty, had to be "done," but over all pre-
vailed an irresistibly jolly air, like children playing
dressing-up at a party.

It never failed to astonish me that the slight-
boned teenage girls, with their thin, delicate hands
and feet and narrow shoulders, would inevitably
grow into the vast, wide-hipped, shapeless proportions of the older women there. I walked through the
graveyard one day when a group of women were

tidying up in preparation for the Bishop's forthcoming visit. They had painted the crib-like palings around the graves white, and smacked cheerful daubs of red and blue on the pointed ends and the arms of the crosses. Now they were busy with axes, hacking and chopping at roots and bushes. They were on the crest of the rise as I came along the path below, and I shall never forget the sight of that row of six full-skirted gargantuan rears presented to me as their owners bent over, made all the more formidable by the six pairs of knee-length fawn Pendleton bloomers anchoring woollen stockings at bulging knees. Nobody could give me an adequate reason for this remarkable structural change. The Indian does not overeat, as this is seldom economically possible, and, although they consume vast quantities of candies (they come up by the ton-load on the tractor-train in winter) I don't think this alone could account for it, as the children eat the most, and there are no fat children, just children whose teeth are unfortunately beginning to show the results.

The graveyard was a remarkably pleasant place. I spent a lot of time there, feeling that this is one of the few places in a small community where a stranger may potter around, stand and stare, or just sit, without arousing speculation or suspicion. So, whenever I felt I wanted to do nothing reasonably, I headed there. (Purposeless activity is unknown to

the Indian — if he goes from A to B it is for a reason, even if the reason is to see whether the ice still
looks the same as it did yesterday; and, if he stands
and stares, it is because he can see better what is
going on; and, should he happen to be beneath the
bough, it is for the very good reason of shade or
shelter.) There seemed to be no boundaries to this
particular graveyard. It wandered higgledy-
piggledy over the hillside and on either side of the
path leading to the church and village, reappearing
unexpectedly in the adjacent gardens of the rectory
and weather station. The graves were placed as haphazardly, each one surrounded with the traditional
high wooden crib, sized according to the occupant.
At the head of each stood a white, wooden cross, almost always with a name painted on it in the syllabic characters common to Cree and Ojib, and sometimes within the crib was a little cross outlined in
white pebbles or shells. Tall spruce grew there on
the sheltered side of the island, and there was a
plank seat for wearied knitters on the brow of the
hill, with a magnificent view over the lake or across
the village. Kill-deers nested there and ran between
the graves, dragging their broken wings along the
ground before me and crying plaintively. Vesper
and song sparrows sang joyously, and children ran
through it on their way to school. The Lands and
Forests officials had to cross it to get to their out-

house. Village dogs sunned themselves, fought and gambolled. It was the most cheerful, active grave-yard I have haunted. No marble tears, no withered flowers or unctuous writings to distract.

History was written there, from the appalling numbers of tiny cribs of the early dates, gradually becoming fewer and fewer up the years to the present day, in tribute to the health services; from the mass grave of those who had drowned from their overturned canoe, to that of the family of five who were drowned when the plane they had chartered to take them to a distant trapline foundered in the lake. There was even history to be traced in the Christian names. Although the sonorous biblical ones still predominated, Jonah and Rebecca, Amos and Martha, Sarah and Ezekiel, there had been a gradual infiltration of outside influence. There were Victorias, Alberts and Edwards, Marlenes and Garys, and some unknown popular influence called Gene-vieve (pronounced "jellybean" in local circles). Here was the decimating year of the influenza epidemic, there, that of the measles . . . but there was no obsequious sorrow here, only an outward adaptation of Christian practises over the age-long acceptance of the Ojibwa that there is a time for living and a time for dying, as cyclically inevitable in man as in all nature around him. Before the coming of the white man and the submission to his deco-

rums, the body in death was of as little account as a
fallen leaf or tree, and as little entitled therefore to a
memorial. The spirit wandered happily, as was its
right, across paradisical hunting grounds teeming
with game and fish, stocked by Kitchemanitou, the
Great Spirit, for his beloved people. Equally happily, all those who remained celebrated their dead in
an annual fest "of great jollity."

The graveyard at Big Trout reflected the overall
impression of the village. It was a community that
was proud of its church and took an active personal
interest in it. There were no offerings of personal
effects to accompany the spirit on its wanderings; no
brooches or toys, no tobacco, surreptitiously tucked
under bouquets of artificial flowers, no coloured ribbons hanging from the crosses. I have seen them in
other communities where the thin veneer of Christianity cracks occasionally under the weight of
death or birth;* in others, the first compromise between pagan mind and Christian burial custom may
be seen in the little houses inside the enclosure containing small effects, money, or treasures (the door
is always open so that the spirit can come and go).

---

* They are today's equivalent of the ". . . warclubs, bows and
arrows, Robes of fur, and pots and kettles. And with food that
friends had given," about which the poor defenceless dead
complained so bitterly:

> "Ay! Why do the living," said they,
> Lay such heavy burdens on us?"
> — LONGFELLOW, *Hiawatha*

Big Trout was also unusual in that it only had one church. Usually there are at least two — Anglican, Roman Catholic, or United, all three having a long established missionary history here and, up to recent times, providing the only education available for Indians. Sometimes various other sects move in as well, but, for the most part, they are not concerned with the physical welfare of the people (which has long been the primary concern of the three established churches) but with the expounding of some private dogma of their own.

I wandered around the white clapboard church one day. The interior was impressive in its simplicity. The altar cross was covered in white beadwork, with a thin interior cross of coloured beads. Apart from the pulpit and lectern hangings, which were exquisitely wrought in an intricate design of beadwork flowers, the only other note of colour was the three-fold *sanctus* painted in red and blue Cree symbols on the chancel arch:

ᑫᐋᐣᑊᐤᐧᑊᕆᒐᐣᔅ

On the wall was a plaque to the memory of "James Melville Harrison of Lincolnshire, also Jeremiah McKay and Peter Cromarty who were accidentally drowned at Trout Lake Post while serving with the

Hudson's Bay Company, aged 21, 15, and 12." The parish notices were all in Cree — the minister has a typewriter with the syllabic forms on the keys instead of letters — and so was a letter from the bishop to his parishioners.

I think that any minister or priest who has worked among the people of this territory will admit that pagan custom and belief lie very lightly submerged, whatever the outward trappings; that an inherent superstition is responsible for many interracial misunderstandings; and that shamans, conjurers or medicine men, professed or unprofessed, still occupy places of power and respect in many communities.

I once asked a Roman Catholic priest on another reserve how he reconciled this knowledge within the spiritual tenets of his church, having just heard that one of the most outwardly pious members of his congregation was a frequent furtive visitor to the cabin of the local mystery man. It was easy, he said. He just prayed twice as hard for such people as he did for anyone else! And anyway, he added, almost echoing the answer of the Anglican minister to whom I put the same question, the most important thing was that these half-way people recognised among the confusions of their emergence into the white world that there was one common defined security for all people; and that all wise parents made allowances for children, and did not try to push their understanding beyond their capacity.

The white people who were probably most in contact with every other aspect of Indian life in every corner of that scattered community were the nurses. Lew and Marg at the nursing station were two of those fiercely independent, outgoing, generous characters that represent the finest in Australian exports, and are to be found in all unlikely corners of the world. They ran a midwifery unit as well, and were responsible for the health of all the settlements for a hundred miles and more around; Fort Severn on Hudson Bay, Kasabonica, Bearskin and Sachigo, flying in on monthly rounds, setting up clinics in the schoolrooms, and whenever there was room on an aircraft (i.e., about six square inches) they would take one or the other, or sometimes both of us.

Both strong as men, they were fishing fanatics in their spare time, and whenever they could get away from the incessant knocking at the nursing station door they took off in their large and powerful motorboat *Digger*, accompanied by their equally large and powerful husky, Kim. (Kim had been AWOL during the winter for many weeks, and they had given him up for lost when he returned one day, jumping out of the aircraft in which he had been flown back from Pickle Crow, about three hundred miles south. One of the pilots who knew him had spotted him in a tavern there, enjoying a bowl of beer with some of the crew of the tractor train, which makes its long lurching journey across the frozen land during the winter, carrying the year's supplies. He must have followed it from Big Trout.) Both nurses loved dogs, and regularly fed some of the starving pack of dogs on the island, yet it was Lew who had taken a gun that spring and shot the winter's pack. A child had been badly mauled, and she warned the villagers that, however unusual such an attack was, the next instance might be fatal, and asked their co-operation in killing off the unclaimed dogs who were only left to starve to death anyway. But there were no volunteers, for it is the rare Ojibwa who will kill any dog outright, or even drown unwanted puppies. Lew borrowed a gun and, with the assistance of a visiting welfare officer, tackled the sickening task herself.

Marg was the quieter one, whose occasional utterances carried considerable weight. Lew was energy translated into human form, the ebullient personality in navy blue slacks and parka, who jumped out of a plane almost before it had tied up and strode purposefully up the dock of whichever outlying settlement she was visiting, marshalling the awaiting inhabitants as she came. I think of her now as we followed in her wake at Bearskin: "Everyone who can walk to the schoolroom, AT THE DOUBLE!"

she boomed cheerfully. "And that goes for you too, Ezekiel Cutfoot —" her eye lighting on a small fearful figure trying to burrow out of sight in its mother's skirts. "And you, too, my poppet —" sweeping up some sloe-eyed toddler with a smacking kiss on its sticky cheek, and "Heaven help you, Ruby Crow, if I don't see you, you bad girl —" with a hearty smack on some grandmother's voluminous rump. And like giggling delighted sheep, understanding her words only by the tone of her voice, the patients were driven before her into the schoolroom. Here she would swiftly set up business, with all her paraphernalia, including an impressive array of dental instruments — her pride and joy was a pair of grisly-looking things called "elevator forceps" — spread over the schoolteacher's desk, and a cot borrowed from the trading post.

I knitted away like Madame Defarge in one corner, while Susan sketched proceedings in another, and in a third the young bearded schoolteacher, an amateur artist, sketched her. Until at one point we all changed positions, Lew commandeering my reluctant shrinking person to point a flashlight down the cavern of a mouth in which her forceps were busy with a stubborn tooth, Susan then circling us like a jackal with busy recording pencil, the schoolteacher close at her heels. And when it was over, the patient, a boy of about seventeen who had retained a total stoic silence throughout the ordeal, and I sat side by side to recover, and I don't know which looked greener.

Lew saw over eighty patients that day, ranging from a wholesale BCG vaccination of the school-children to young Master Beardy in a cowboy hat, a comforter in his mouth, and the as yet unpumped-up contents of a bottle of aspirin in his stomach. She worked her way through burns and booster shots, running ears and eczema, pregnancy, piles and Potts fractures, pausing only for a cup of coffee and some cold sausages, a bag of which always accompanied her on her trips. Hepatitis was rampant in the village, and even as she was waiting for the interpreter to relay the reply to some diagnostic question she would be catching up on the laboratory test of the patient before. ("Run back to the wig-wam, love," she would say, "and bring me back a specimen," and back they came with her request in some of the most unusual laboratory containers: rusty cans, pop bottles, and one that brought the house down when Lew turned her caustic wit upon it and inquired how the miracle had been performed — a plastic bottle of the detergent-dispenser type, with a hole the size of a pin-head.) She scolded and praised, sympathised and snapped, and seemed to have an encyclopaedic knowledge of the names, numbers and circumstances of every family. Woe

betide the mother who had neglected to bring her
fifth in for its booster shot, or the father who had not
brought his son back from the fishing camp for his
routine TB check. She dispensed pills and vitamins,
short shrift for malingerers, and endless patience.
"Two 3tds." scribbles a doctor on his prescription
pad, which being interpreted means "2 teaspoon-
fuls, three times daily," but was prescribed by Lew
with a teaspoon in one hand and two fingers up-
raised in the other: "When the sun is up — *two*"
she said, pouring herself an imaginary dose, and
gulping it down for good measure. "When the sun
is up here" (pointing to the ceiling with her spoon)
— "*two;* when the sun goes down — *two*, you understand?" Gabble, gabble, gabble between interpreter and patient. "She says, what if it is raining
and she cannot see the sun —" said the interpreter
with a perfectly straight face. "Dear God," said Lew
absently, already busy with the next patient, "tell
her to take an educated guess!"

There are few, if any, fullblooded Ojibwa or
Cree, even here in this most isolated territory where
one might reasonably expect to find them. At Bearskin that afternoon, I was looking across at the row
of patients waiting and was startled to see so many
faces of unmistakable Celtic origin that no amount
of dark pigmentation of skin or straight black hair
could disguise, and was not surprised to hear that

the surnames of many of them sounded like a rallying of the clans. Sometimes I thought I detected other hereditary traits — a sly, pawky humour that on the surface seemed bland and inoffensive enough, but sometimes planted a shrewd barb of insidious doubt that left one uneasily wondering whether it was one's own unworthy interpretation or the product of a mind that was considerably wilier than one had thought . . . and a mind, what is more, that thoroughly enjoyed putting the White Man in his place.

And I thought of all the outside pressures that were brought to bear upon the Indian today, and decided that a mental make-up like this would be the only and inevitable defence of a once proud and independent people if they had any hope at all of retaining some of their individuality — an outward acceptance of the white man's often illogical laws and seemingly bottomless coffers, and a retreating afterwards to the privacy of their tipis to laugh like mad over them, then turn all their ingenuity to subtleties of exploitation and circumvention. And this, I thought with affectionate family pride, is just how some of their ancestors dealt with the occupying Sassenach after the '45. . . . But common sense reminded me that the Scots had time on their side to play their canny waiting game. They were not caught up in a madly accelerated race of atomic

progress; the world was still vast beneath unbroken sonic barriers, its population still naturally balanced with fire and pestilence, war and famine. While these present-day occupiers, the nurses, the ministers and priests, schoolteachers, agents and welfare officers, were all there on socio-economic reasons directed to the ultimate benefit of the occupied territory. All were altruistic representatives of a government desperately trying to make up for social and territorial injustices (to those "whose aboriginal interest in the soil of Upper Canada must be extinguished") often committed centuries ago in an understandable ignorance of the direction of world events. Now they must cross bridges of ethnological adjustment long before they have properly got to them, with the twin taunts of discrimination and procrastination always snapping at their heels, in their almost slap-happy haste to rush their aboriginal children out of childhood, through the developing pangs of puberty and into the full social and civic maturity of a Just Society already overburdened with problems of poverty and unemployment.

Meanwhile, as the natural economy of fishing and trapping will no longer support the burgeoning population, they must supplement with spoonfed welfare gruel — that deadly insidious staple for which aboriginal children the world over develop such a taste that eventually they wish for nothing else. And even if they do not, soon there will be no alternative.

I wish I knew the answer. So, I expect, do harassed governments the world over. I only know that I wished that day at Bearskin that a Brigadoon-like mist might descend, leaving these brown-skinned Scots forever unaware of what lay beyond.

Time passed at Big Trout — too quickly, and soon we were into the idyllic days of a northern June, that brief time between the break-up of ice and the advent of the first man-eating mosquito and black fly, when suddenly one day the birch and poplar open the first full tender green of leaves, and all the birds are paired off. The air is pungent with wood fires smoking and tanning, damp thawing earth and spagnum moss. There is a new strange melodious moment reached at the peak of the village dogs' howling; washing tubs are brought outside, and old people sit once more in the sun by the cabin door.

Most of the time, Susan and I went our separate ways during the day. I pottered peacefully around the island, content to absorb without effort, sometimes in the company of children, mostly alone, and always with an assortment of the roving dogs. Susan's professional contentment lay in the growing stack of paintings and her determination to record every facet of life there, from the people and their occupations to the details of the embroidery on a

carrying bag, to the exact procedure for skinning a
beaver or gutting a fish. The combination of my
blotting-paper assimilation of the life around me
and her factual observation could not have been better, for when we met over one of our primitive but
filling meals in the shack we would often find that
each had something to add to the other's accounts of
the same thing. Mostly she found that her pencil
and pad were sufficient entrée into any cabin or tent,
and the people forthcoming and relaxed about sitting for her, but very occasionally she encountered
opposition, such as a determined turning away from
an older woman, or William, who refused to be
sketched for he "would not have his likeness nailed
to a wall," or Ezekial, who had a particularly arresting face (with the additional attraction of the rumoured powers of a shaman), who had not left his
cabin for days, and refused to open the door, because "he had seen a windigo." A windigo is a can-
nibal spirit.

We did not always eat in our customary squalor
— the justly famous northern hospitality saw to
that, with ambrosial meals of sturgeon, speckled
trout and pickerel cheeks, goose marinated in mar-
malade and caribou in wine. Because it was such a
small self-contained community we were drawn into
it, with a constant coming and going to and from
our shack, both white people and Indians, so that we

came to know almost everyone on the island. Armed with sketchbook or knitting we found our way into cabin or canvas matagwan to meet perhaps Rebecca's sloe-eyed Baby Bunting, wrapped in his rabbit-skin blanket, swaying dreamily in a minute hammock suspended from the lodge poles. Or Maria, with a bead headband on her hand loom, the tiny coloured beads heaped in a bowl beside her, the needle darting in and out of the heap as accurately as a woodpecker's beak to skewer the pattern colours, then shuttling through the narrow strings. Or Lucy's seemingly ancient mother, sitting dumpy and crosslegged in her tent, her face a network of fine wrinkles, but her hands, those small finely boned Indian hands, young and smooth, busy with moccasins; or Genevieve scraping beaver skins or kneading moosehide. While outside one might stop and talk to one of the men, caulking a canoe or mending nets and traps or fashioning a snowshoe; or to little boys with improbable names like Gary Eaglestick or Chiefie Ottertail, fishing off the dock, shooting alleys or sawing wood . . . theirs was the shy, childlike friendliness of a people who laughed easily — with us and not at us. When we left, some of the women we had come to know especially well came down to see us off with gifts and moccasins and miniature doll-sized mukluks.

We flew back in the Cessna, crammed in more

than ever with freshly painted canvases, parcels to post for our friends, the bearskin, snowshoes, more moccasins, and about twenty pounds of speckled trout on ice — the pride of my fishing life, from an unexpected trip to the Pippewasin River on Hudson Bay the day before. And a papoose — Linda Lillian, no less, her round dark cheeks flushed with fever, her black eyes wide and wondering. She was laced up in a neat parcel in an apapasian, the spagnum moss-lined bag that fits inside the outer lacings of the tikkinagan, and looked for all the world like an Indian doll in a handcraft shop. Linda Lillian had pneumonia, she was labelled for the Indian Hospital at Sioux Lookout, and we were to deliver her there. She was our parting present from the nursing station, and we got to know her rather well. Not to worry, said Lew, seeing our apprehension, she'll sleep the whole way. She didn't. We ran into a terrible storm and had to fly miles and hours off course to skirt it, forced so low that I could almost read the expression in the eye of an eagle perched on top of a spruce. It was rough. Linda Lillian was terrified and lost in this lurching, noisy world and cried without ceasing, finding no comfort in our strange white faces. Even John, most imperturbable of pilots, began to look a little strained. Eventually, in the last of twilight, we came down at Pickle Crow, the little gold mine town. By now we were thor-

oughly alarmed at the baby's rapid rasping breathing and hot dry skin, but by chance there was a male
nurse on duty that night at the mine hospital and he
took her in. We spent the night in the creaking
wooden hotel, from the beer parlour of which, directly below our room, emerged in an unsteady
steady stream many black-haired, dark-faced people,
men and women, with wildly glazed unfocussing
eyes — the representatives of Linda Lillian's race
who were already emergent into the full freedom
and benefits of the white man's civilisation; and
were constitutionally unable to deal with them. I
knew, listening to the voices outside, that tonight
could easily fall into the pattern so monotonously
apparent in the magistrate's court — a fight, a beat-
ing-up perhaps, even a stabbing. These, then, would
be the people by whom the outside world would
judge the Indian people as a whole; few would ever
know the ones who had gone quietly home that
night; few would ever know the gentle, quiet, courteous people of Big Trout, in their own setting, still
only halfway across the span of centuries between us.

Linda Lillian was restored to us next morning, a
now more tranquil — and decidedly more fragrant
— bundle, her breathing considerably easier. She
cried only briefly as we took off, then seemed to re-
sign herself to the inevitable.

I looked down on her as she lay in my arms before we handed her over at Sioux Lookout, and she gazed back at me with huge unhappy eyes. She was only six months old and she had come a long way. It would be Linda Lillian's generation who would cross the bridge between our cultures; there was so much for her to do and learn before then, so much to hope for . . . She looked very small, and very defenceless. I wished her well with all my heart.

5

Spring Days at Sandy Lake

S ANDY LAKE is in the Northwest, about one hundred and seventy miles west of Big Trout, not far from the border of Manitoba, the outlying components that make up its band scattered around a wide area at Sachigo, Deer Lake and Favourable Lake. Its people are noted for their friendliness, and when Susan and I were invited to stay at the nursing station on the main settlement and enjoy all the blessings of real plumbing and beds, we promptly made plans to arrive in early June, as soon as the ice had gone out from the lake.

Susan, who has transit problems and always primes herself beforehand on soporific Gravol, immediately fell asleep in the rear cockpit of the

Beaver, her head resting on a sack of distributive
clothing, her feet on a paper bag containing a roast
of beef and six pounds of sausages. I sat in front
with Nollie the pilot, with whom we had both flown
on other trips; as conversation had to be conducted
in a roar above the noise of the engine, I soon
croaked into silence and was content to look down
over the endless mosaic of dark land and glinting
water that makes up the northern coniferous forest
zone — spruce, balsam and jackpine, with here and
there a sprinkling of birch and poplar and mountain
ash, although as yet there was only a faint green
promise to mark the deciduous trees; outcrops of
smooth Precambrian granite, and gneiss; and, almost in equal areas to the land, the steel grey mono-
chromes to varying blues of the lakes, sometimes
stained in yellow abstract patterns from the clay.
There were masses of low-lying clouds building up
to the northwest, occasionally shot through with
lightning, and Nollie altered course quite frequently
to skirt the storm.

Once in the distance we saw a bolt hit the ground
and almost immediately there was a rising plume of
smoke: we had actually witnessed the start of a forest fire. We altered course again to fly over it and,
godlike, looked down on the tongues of orange
flame, licking greedily and ever more swiftly
through the underbrush and up into the branches of

the trees, soon to leap up into roaring life and sweep over the land until halted by some vagary of wind or water. This fire, in a desolate area of scrubby trees, would be left to burn itself out. Only if it got really out of hand would Indians from the nearest settlements be recruited and flown in as fire-fighters — a job for which they have a singular aptitude, with their innate knowledge of bush conditions.

After two hours' flying, only fifty miles from Sandy, visibility suddenly closed in, so that Nollie decided to make for Pikangikum nearby, a small reserve, whose band forms part of the Sandy Lake territory for administrative and health purposes, and await the clearing there. Susan and I were delighted anyway, as we had heard a good deal about Pikangikum and read R.W. Dunning's ethnographic study.* Its people seemed to be different from even their near neighbours (originally they were part of the Little Grand Rapids Band in Manitoba), both physically and in their still withdrawn and isolated attitude to the other components of the band. Also they had an interesting history of shamanism — conjuring, tent shaking, sweat lodges, etc., long after it had ceased to exist — officially anyway — elsewhere; and, until quite recently, their Treaty Day parties had been bang-up affairs, with a feast

* R. W. Dunning, *Social and Economic Change Among the Northern Ojibwa*, 2 vols. (University of Toronto Press, 1959).

and a drum dance, and ceremonial pipes smoked
with the agent.

So we circled and came in through the clouds to
sudden dazzling sunshine, and even though we were
unexpected there was the usual inexplicable turnout
of the population at the end of the dock to watch our
arrival. The difference in appearance was immediately clear; for one thing they seemed on first impression to be of a slimmer build, with finer, nar-
rower features. The women wore their hair in a
distinctive style — long and straight to the shoulders, except for the side opposite the parting which
was looped back into a flat pad and fixed there with
a barrette, plastic or beaded; and one or two combs
on the top of the head secured the downward fall of
the back hair. All wore ankle length skirts, even the
girls and toddlers, and their eyes were shy and
downcast compared to their cousins of Sandy, who
look directly at one, and whose mouths are always
ready to break into a smile.

We wandered separately along the trails to the
nursing station, Susan heading with her sketchbook
for the log school in search of small subject material, and I, inevitably, for the graveyard on the hill.
Among the weathered wooden cribs of the random
gravesites I found a fairly recent one of a child,
quite openly pagan: inside the small palisade of the
tri-pointed wooden stakes sat a little lodge with slop-

ing roof. There was, it was true, a cross at one end, but from the cross hung strings of beads, and on the threshold of the doorless entrance lay a Christmas cracker brooch and a small pink plastic purse. Further on, in a clearing off the cedar log trail through the woods, was the small frame building which was the United Church, and nearby an elderly man was piling logs; the pastor of this church, a Cree, who had worked as a missionary in the North for nearly fifty of his seventy years. "There are three churches in Pikangikum," he told me, "and no real Christians." I asked which predominated in numbers of congregation, Catholic, United or the more recent Pentecostal? "Whichever offers the most at the moment," was his reply, not sad or cynical, but matter-of-fact.

With mugs of tea and sandwiches we sat outside the nursing station. Now the sun poured down from a cloudless sky and it was hot — 76° — yet over at Sandy the low cloud ceiling was still impenetrable, Nollie informed us, fresh off the radio. We could be socked in for hours or even days, so swiftly changing are local weather conditions; but time had already ceased to have any urgency for us, so that we were able to sink into the peaceful cyclical timelessness here without giving the matter a thought. Unfortunately we couldn't do any further exploration in case Nollie suddenly decided to leap into the Beaver and take off. I lay back, a warm, sleepy and contented sheep, and gazed up through the bare poplar branches to the now clear and lucid blue; it seemed incredible that the ice went out only a day or two ago; even as I looked it seemed that there was a hint of green among the branches, so swiftly does spring turn to summer here.

A quarter of an hour later, just as I was about to drop off, a voice on the radio within said crackle screech screech crackle; Nollie drained his coffee cup and headed for the dock. By magic the population had already materialized there by the time we reached it. Half an hour later the clouds cleared as we circled lower, and suddenly there, in a clearing reaching from the dark forested area to the lake-shore, were the toy buildings of Sandy Lake, the steeple of the church glinting in the sun, flags fluttering from the tall white staffs before the nursing station and the Hudson's Bay post, and a clearly defined web of trails through the surrounding bush.

As we taxied up to the dock, Willie the caretaker came hirpling along to hold a wing, his face one broad welcoming smile. His gait was crablike for he had the congenital hip displacement so common among the people of Sandy — although Willie was more unfortunate than most in having both hips afflicted, it was remarkable how little handicapped he was, for he sped up the rocks, laden with our gear, like a mountain goat, and we were almost running, trying to keep up with him. He was as nimble and agile in the boat.

Nowadays it is only adults one sees with the typical rolling up-and-down gait (I still retain a vivid impression of a group of four people walking in single file, silhouetted against a rise of land, and looking like some strange mammoth centipede, for the first, or head, was normal, but the last three, the legs, were afflicted, but on alternate hips), as the children are flown out nowadays to the Sick Children's Hospital in Toronto for remedial surgery. Willie's youngest daughter, Ida, had recently returned from such a sojourn, and it was impossible to distinguish her from any other normal active eight-year-old, except, unfortunately, in the hospital-acquired pertness she now displayed towards her elders, Indian and white alike. There seems little doubt that with a hereditary hip weakness like this the universal use of the tikkanagan, or carrying board, is a contributory factor: the child with perhaps a borderline condition being snugly immobilised in the worst possible position with straight extended legs, then continually carried or propped upright in a vertical position so that even gravity must work against it.

We were in clover, for Mary Houghton, the nurse, could not have been more welcoming and

hospitable; and what was more she loved to cook
and was a cook supreme. The housework was done
by Maida, who also assisted Mary with patients and
did the interpreting, in the office and two-bed sick
bay at the far end of the ranch style building. Here
the radio crackled away much of the day, unheard,
unheeded — until by some unconscious reaction it
apparently became instantly meaningful to Maida
or Mary, wherever they were, when it concerned
Sandy Lake. Here, if one had a mind to, one could
sit all day and learn all the gossip and activities for
hundreds of miles around — a party of Americans
telephoning out from some outfitter's fishing camp
on the Berens River to Cleveland, New York, San
Francisco; geologists on a field trip maintaining
touch with one another; a drowning at God's Lake
and the radio machinery now being set in motion to
fly in a police skin diver; a pilot requesting local
weather conditions (at this Mary cocked an eye at
the sky over the lake and said that the ceiling was
one, two or three, or whatever it seemed to her, thousand feet); the hospital, the bishop — the list was
endless.

The windows of my comfortable (catalogue-
furnished and brought up by the tractor-train in
winter) bedroom looked down from this height of
land over the great expanse of lake with its low,
jagged-treeline horizon, deserted now save for the

occasional canoe or boat putt-putting past, their gunwales low in the water. It was Treaty Day time again, time to return from the traplines, clothes washing time, reunion time, and a time of much coming and going between the Hudson's Bay post and the rival Northwest Trader's — first to change the pelts for cash or credit, and then to take it all out again in clothes and food and equipment.

I walked along the cedar boardwalk from the station compound, over the hill and down to the open grassy slopes below, where the shingle and log buildings of church, school and rectory were dotted about. Where the boardwalk ended, the path turned to clogging clay morasses as the sun melted the frost, and rubber boots or galoshes pulled over one's mocassins were essential. It was much warmer on this side, for the bay is sheltered, and I propped myself against an oil drum on the dock and watched the world go by — full-skirted women with tikkanagans on their backs, on their way to the Bay or the nursing station, purposeful men with haversacks, young girls in incongruous — but practical — stretch pants, two or three young bucks, in boots of winkle-picker pointedness and very white shirts. They very seldom talked as they walked. All around were the sounds of an Indian village on a spring morning: lake water lapping, and the scream of diving terns, a dog howling, the sweet clarity of a vesper sparrow piercing brilliantly through the harsh conversation of two ravens — and somewhere far off a buzz saw shrilled. To all this presently was added children's voices, pitched to a universal released-to-recess level; and nearer at hand the deeper voices of Father Dumont and two helpers as they pulled down a log shack (carefully extracting any nails for re-use), and piled the lumber. Father Dumont was the French Canadian Oblate missionary here, and he had provided Susan with a studio in the shape of a storage shed. This was handily situated near the dock and just beside the well-worn path from the village, so that she never lacked for subjects, and as the days went by and more canvases leaned against the walls or charcoal portraits were pinned up, one and all wandered through as though at an art gallery, giggling over likenesses of friends and relations. Here, visiting her later on, I met Barrie, the junior teacher of the R.C. school — a Micmac from Nova Scotia, and a most delightful enthusiastic youngster. He left as the other teacher arrived, one Rudi, who was part American Sioux and part Italian, and who somewhat stunned the inhabitants when he first arrived by appearing in leotards — watching his turned-out-toe, almost mincing Malvolio approach, I was not altogether surprised. He had with him Arthur, a twelve-year-old Swampy Cree whom he introduced as his "ward" from Saskatchewan and whose presence here was causing much disquietude among those who had the welfare of children at heart, for no one seemed quite able to account for a Treaty Indian child from Saskatchewan being brought to an Ontario reserve by an American teacher. One gathered that so intricate was the inter-provincial legislation, so many the departments involved, that no one had quite known how to go about unravelling the unfortunate Arthur in the past few months, and in the meantime the red hot pins were passed quickly from one pair of hands to the other so that no one would be held responsible for the first official thread pulled . . . Arthur looked wretched.

I returned to my oil drum to brood. There are some influences our emergent Indians can do without in Canada and right at the moment I would have put Rudi at the head of my list. He was a trouble-maker who had brought some of the murkier aspects of the white man's world to this unsophisticated land, along with his movie camera, projector and various unsavoury reels of film; he had undermined by doubt and confusion that very day a class of children, bursting in upon a period of religious instruction and telling them that they should not go to confession; he had the wretched Arthur; he had . . . (However, unbeknownst, as the cliffhanger novelist school used to say, the mills of the provin-

cial gods were grinding slowly but surely Down
East, and the end of Rudi was at hand —).

Because I had listened to so many discussions —
sparked off by the plight of Arthur — in the last
few days concerning Indian foster children, adoption practises and similar problems, I resolved to try
and sort some of the facts from the someone-told-me
legends. There was a particularly disturbing account that I had heard many times concerning a
planeload of children sent up from the Children's
Aid for placement, either adoptive or as foster children. Those families who had put their names down
for a child — and many which had not — went
down to meet them at the dock and take their choice.
No one in any position of responsibility or knowledge, ministers, teachers, or nurse, was consulted as
to the desirability or background of the applicants;
no official came to inspect. Undoubtedly most of
those children would eventually be happier in their
new families than in the sterile restrictive atmosphere of an orphanage, for Indian families are generously expandable to the orphans and strays of
their own people, and cases of neglect and cruelty
almost unheard of. But equally undoubtedly there
were a few cases where the role of the child was one
of hardworking unpaid servant; and one case at
least where the child ran away, and in dangerous
sub-zero temperatures. Plenty of Indian children,

like children the world over, run away from school.
It is the desperately unhappy child that tries to run
back to school. We have done so much with our
Children's Welfare services; there are most rigour-
ous and exacting requirements for the adoption of a
white child, yet sometimes when it comes to the
adoption of our Indian children I cannot help feeling
there is only too often simply a sigh of official relief
at placing a child anywhere.

I walked on up through the village, the haphaz-
ard collection of log cabins and shacks, where much
spring activity was going on, with families moving
into the summer quarters, for many of them still
maintain their nomadic tradition — the winter
quarters being smaller, easier to heat, and further
back from the lake. Children raking, mothers sitting
on the steps before washtubs, their babies gravely
surveying the passing world from the upright cra-
dleboards, the washing lines bowed under the
weight of dancing clothes and bright quilts, and
over all the smell of woodsmoke. Well out of reach
of hungry roaming dogs, snowshoes were cached on
roofs or platforms, the long narrow northern snowshoes, their frames made from two ribs of wood,
tacked or bound together at the ends. I said "B'zoi,"
or "Watchi!" and everybody smiled back, and
laughed with me at my labourious attempts to dis-
cuss the weather.

One evening Father Dumont came for dinner; short and stocky, unworldly, yet with the great dispassionate love and understanding of his people that seems to be the hallmark of every Oblate father that I have met. Last winter in his rectory, which is heated only by a wood stove (oil would be too expensive for his budget), there had been many nights when he could not get the temperature above anything between fourteen and thirty degrees, even although he rose four and five times during the night to stoke the fire. We played some lamentable bridge, and afterwards he taught me the Cree syllabic symbols by the simplest method I had yet seen, and we read from my Cree grammar which has a strange insistence upon *mowe* — the verb to eat — pages and pages being devoted to it in all tenses and forms ranging from the indignant "thou didst eat me" to the complacent "when I shall have eaten him." "I eat myself" offered some speculation as to where one would start — the toes seemed the obvious place, but none of us were supple enough to put our feet in our mouths. Susan wondered whether it would ever be worth her while to learn *mow-ittonanewan* on the off-chance that she might want to observe to someone that "people are eating each other." The grammar was written in 1881 by a missionary Bishop of Moosanee, which probably explains the choice of this verb as a model instead of the more normal "to love," so many missionary bishops having perished universally in the pots of gourmet flocks. I suggested this to Father Dumont, and, ideal audience that he was, he laughed until the last button popped off his threadbare jacket, and I felt like Stephen Leacock, Mark Twain and Sydney Smith rolled into one.

Susan and I went to Sunday morning service in his little church, whose steeple soared from pink shingles on the skyline. The service was conducted in Cree, but it was easy for us to join in the singing and responses with Cree hymn and prayer books as the words are pronounced just as they are written. The tunes were familiar but the timing dragged somewhat, the singing dominated by Moses Kakapetum, a counsellor. As I stood there singing, most of the time I knew not what, almost overwhelmed by the stuffy smell of humanity as yet unwashed from the winter's cold, and of moccasins and old hymn books, I felt a small insistent tugging at my laces: a very small sloe-eyed bundle had crawled under the pew and was busily trying to take off my shoes. I smiled down at it, and the corners of its mouth were just turning up in response when it disappeared, soundlessly, like a Cheshire cat — dragged backwards over the floor into the maternal arms in the pew behind. There was no whimper of protest, no indignant foiled wail, as there might be from a

white baby: Indian children are greatly indulged,
yet they seldom cry as a spoiled white child would. I
turned my attention to Moses, looking thoughtful,
bland and pious in his steel spectacles; I wished I
knew what ticked behind them. I had met him the
previous day with Norval Morriseau, the Ojibwa
artist, and Chief Tom Fiddler; he had acted as interpreter when the chief decided it was one of the days
he couldn't speak English. Feeling that it was only
courteous to explain my presence on his reserve,
even although I was Mary's guest, I had told him
that I was a writer, and that I was here to get on
with my work, because here I could find the necessary conditions of remote peace and freedom from
interruption. The chief looked sceptical, and I
wasn't surprised, as Moses had managed to con-
dense my explanation into four words, one of which,
kispin, I recognised as being "if." I spent the rest of
the sermon wondering what the other words were.
"If uninterrupted will write," "if writer I'm Dutch-
man" "*writes* — if you please!" and before I knew
it we were standing up singing the last hymn.

Later I asked Father Dumont the meaning of
some words more than usually repetitive that I had
jotted down — *misquam* was one. "Ice," he said,
and it had occurred so frequently because he was
using the metaphor of "snow, ice and steam" to explain the Trinity as fundamentally as possible: all

different, yet one element. And the impassioned first part of his sermon, I asked, where he got so carried away every time he used a word that sounded like *ahseega* that I had decided it must be some sort of sin. He laughed: the first part of the "sermon" had consisted of parish notices, he said, and as for "*ahseega*," it was his dock, presently floating, and he was warning the children to keep off it at this dangerous time of year, and warning the parents at the same time. "If I did not repeat the warning many times," he said, "they would not think I really meant it."

Later, we walked across the peninsula to visit Norval Morriseau. He and his family were visiting the reserve, living in a cabin in the woods for several months, where the demands of his recent spectacular successes would be less exacting than among his own people at Beardmore, near Lake Nipigon, or in the city where we had last seen him. There was one bare room with a stove, a table and several bold-line, legend-interpretive paintings on the walls; one bedroom almost entirely filled with a bed on which at the moment slept the latest Morriseau, a baby of about four months; and one smaller room almost entirely filled with stones, rocks and artifacts, the walls hung with leather pouches, gourds, rattles, and sinister and repulsive figures made from moose hooves, fur, etc. I noticed a Bible with a beautifully beaded cover cheek by jowl with such a figure, and talking with Norval, as he explained some of his more exotic treasures in his usual serio-comic way, we gathered that he was off on a drum cult kick. He appeared to be at outs with Christianity in general at the moment. "Those of us who are lucky have made it, but many of us are still behind because we are trying to live like our white brothers and by their religion, ignoring our great ancestral culture." To this end, presumably, he was planning a slap-up pagan name-giving ceremony for the child instead of a christening, and invited us to it. But to my sorrow we would be gone by the time it took place, for such a ceremony, with a few of Norval's innovations thrown in for good measure, could not fail to be interesting. He looked like a mischievous little boy at the prospect.

Next morning we woke up to two inches of snow, but it soon melted in the sun, leaving a treacherous slush over the already perilous surface. Susan headed for her studio after breakfast, Mary was busy with her morning clinic and office work, but the thought of my typewriter appalled me, so I set off for the village.

Patched tents and tarpaulin shelters were springing up beside the cabins as more and more families arrived for Treaty Day pay-out. Grey-white huskies were chained back in the bush behind the cabins and everywhere there seemed to be the smell of beaver smoking. Most cabins had two or three of the scraped pelts stretched on willow frames up on the roof. The meat was draped on a tripod arrangement of poles over the fire. One bent old crone, with a tartan tam over unexpectedly fuzzy white hair, and shapeless in innumerable skirts, presided like a witch over a fire on which she was smoking sturgeon, and the roe hung in pink clusters, a small fortune in the caviar world, and commonplace here. I stopped and talked to her, and she gave me a piece of fish to try with a nutcracker smile of bared gums. She lived alone at an intersection of the trails in the woods, but a grandchild cut logs for her and brought water.

All along the trails I met little boys, some of them barely more than toddlers, all armed with lethal looking slingshots — which explained the almost total absence of birds immediately around the village. One of them, whom I had watched the day before fishing for sunfish off the dock, accompanied me for a while, and gravely and politely taught me the words for spruce, poplar and birch; *saysaykatuk*, *aseytayah*, and *wekwasaktik*. I asked him to write them for me in my notebook, but he did not know the syllabic writing, and could not spell them in ordinary letters. Susan had already sketched him, he told me, adding guilelessly that she gave him some candies too. I fished in my pockets and found some gumdrops.

I passed a little cemetery by the side of the trail; one child's grave had plastic Woolworth-type toys lying on it, along with a rain-washed but still garishly coloured religious card. Later, meeting Father Dumont, I asked him about the toys. "Yes," he said, "I saw them there — and I will take them away of course, but later, for it is respect that puts them there, and I like to respect their respect." He added the inevitable rider that one hears from all missionaries here, Protestant or Catholic alike, that imported religions still lie very lightly on the surface after even a century's exposure. I went on my way pondering. Part of me is glad that the beautiful complex beliefs evolved from thousands of centuries of a people's ecological development resisted the eternally nagging burden of original sin which the white man's religion heaped upon their moral shoulders, (sin until then was recognized only as a deed that might undermine the delicately balanced survival structure of a band, and not as a miserable personal hypothesis). Part of me is sorry, knowing that some aspects of paganism — such as the powers of a shaman — are better suppressed in a world where big-time racketeers and extortionists appear almost nightly on the television or cinema screen. Even here, in the remote North, there are occasional film

showings in the Community Hall, Westerns mostly,
with the audience naturally cheering on the Savage
Red Hordes, but there are others where some of the
more sinister intricacies of white man's graft might
well provide food for thought to an enterprising
shaman in the audience.

I passed by a shack with "Red Rovers Club"
painted on a drooping sign, and from within I heard
the reassuring sounds of a guitar and much normal,
hoarse teenage laughter.

I was interviewed the following day by Josiah,
seventh-grade student at the R.C. school, for the reserve newspaper *Kitiwin*, (The "*Call*"),

PƆΔ I

at the instigation of his mentor, Rudi. Josiah adjusted his glasses in faithful imitation, and posed
his pencil over the notebook: "Your name?" he
asked briskly, although he knew perfectly well
what it was. "And what best sellers have you written?" As I had only written two books in my life
I was rather at a loss how to answer this without
losing face. "Well, actually . . ." I said, stalling
for time. "How do you spell that?" he asked, and I
spelled out "actually" for him slightly mystified.
"And the next?" said Josiah, assiduously licking

his pencil. "The next was not exactly a best seller," I said, suddenly seeing the light and hoping that he would assume WELL, ACTUALLY was. "NOT EXACTLY A BEST SELLER" he wrote, and I gave up. "That's all," I said, and before his busy pencil would award me THAT'S ALL as a third literary triumph, I said in desperation, "That's all — and I mean that's all — there are only two —" and conscience smiting me I suggested that he let me write the titles down for him. But it was no good; he was scribbling away and I could see that any denial or explanation was only going to swell the list of mythical masterpieces. I was beginning to feel unreal. "Where do you come from?" he now asked, and I told him that I was born in Scotland. "Scotland?" he said, a gratifying tone of recognition in his voice, "Isn't that where Pete Armour comes from?" Pete Armour was the Northwest Trading factor. "Yes," I said, and on a sudden burst of childish irritation I added "But I was born there first!" I craned my neck to see what he was writing: "First born in Scotland." I felt even more nebulous.

And now Josiah turned to the back of his notebook where some numbered questions were written in a different hand. He read the first one through, his lips moving silently, then ticked it off as he repeated it aloud: "What do you think of Indian integration?" and I smelled the unmistakable scent of a

red-grey eminence: this atypical question could only
have been framed by one devious alien mind in
Sandy Lake, and my hackles bristled so that I was
extra careful. "There's nothing to think about — in
Canada," I said. "It's a natural evolvement with no
opposition." (I would have liked to add that the only
opposition here came from some of the village elders, who would do anything in their power to stop
young members of the band from leaving the reserve — not by force as we know it, but by the tribal
force by which the young still obey their elders, even
to the point of submitting to arranged marriages
sometimes — but of course I didn't.) Although I
could hardly control myself when he wrote:
"Doesn't think anything of it."

"And what do you think of the Indian's standard
of living compared to the white man's?" now inquired the hapless Josiah, and I felt my toe itching
for a certain leotard-clad bottom. *Which* white man,
I wanted to ask, the hackneyed plutocrat who has
been driving past in his carriage and pair for centuries, grinding the faces of his less fortunate brothers in the dust as he goes — or the average one who
works hard for his living in the white rat-race to pay
for every benefit you receive for nothing, that unfortunate "Euro-Canadian working like a slave for
fifty weeks of the year in order to spend a fortnight

living as some Indians do the year round;" * or his
brother who lives on the same relief as 75% of the
families of this community, and still doesn't have
free hunting or land to supplement his needs? Or
the white nurse who has the responsibility of the
health of this community, and is paid less than the
caretaker? And . . . but suddenly I remembered
that little human freight load, and knew that I was
as responsible for it as anyone else, that I had no
right to defend my society here. "I feel I am not
qualified to express an opinion," I said, with a fine
evasive humility. "Doesn't know," wrote Josiah —
and for once he was right.

Josiah ticked off the last question: "And what is
your philosophy on life?" he asked, and taking out a
knife he cleaned his nails with such assured thor-
oughness that I found that any philosophy I might
have had was entirely unequal to the present strains
of this interview. I made the supreme effort and
smiled at him; it was not his fault that he was cast in
the role of a Trilby, and I was curious now to find
out if he understood anything of his own questions:
"I tell you what, Josiah," I said, "why don't you try
and guess?" Josiah was momentarily floored. He
considered me obliquely, and looked almost hu-

* *Human Relations*, Ontario Human Rights Commission, vol. 7
(June 1966).

manly shy. "Go on," I encouraged him. "Catho —" he started, then suddenly changed; "no, United?"

"Not quite," I assured him. "Anglican."

When he was gone I looked at the English-edition copies of *Kitiwin* he had left. I noted that the publication was five dollars in debt up to the last publication; however, an anonymous benefactor had promised to clear this debt if the editors promised to keep the paper going for a further twelve months. The two-page broadsheet was filled with references to weddings in which the brides were always described as blushing or nervous, and the grooms as erstwhile bachelors; there were good wishes for families setting out for the spring trapping, or patients being flown out to the Indian hospital at Sioux Lookout. And there were some interesting reports of traffic accidents in this roadless land. Mr. Hopless Beardy, for example, his skidoo pursued by children accelerated and hit a stump. However, "on regaining consciousness, he discovered he had no injuries." Another case of reckless driving occurred when Mr. Parliment Kakapetum crashed into an outhouse, thereby catapulting the embarrassed occupant into a snowbank, or, as the *Kitiwin* delicately described it, "seriously disturbing the occupant who was forced to continue his business elsewhere." The illustrations were done by a talented young Indian artist, his natural talents obviously in-

fluenced by the wham bang ##***!! comic
school. The outhouse scoop was very adequately il-
lustrated: the paper being produced for the first
time with two colours of ink, red and blue, he was
able to make full use of them and produce a very red
Indian's face and a very red behind.

Another headline that puzzled me intermittently
for the rest of the day was MAGGIE FIDDLER GETS
STUCK: "Our roving reporter got an earful on this
very hot item. It seems that Mrs. Maggie Fiddler
got stuck under her bed while searching for her be-
longings. It was a long torturous three hours before
she was rescued by Mrs. Kanette Meekis, who happened to pass by. . . ." "Whew," then comments
the paper, "what a narrow escape."

"Whew" indeed, I thought, but what lay behind
this narrow escape? Whew had it been any other
than Mrs. Kanette Meekis, or whew the possible
consequences if the search for those intriguing be-
longings had been successful? Or even the whew
possibility of Mrs. Fiddler remaining stuck under
bed until reduced, Pooh-like, to retractable proportions? The possibilities were endless, and I found
her returning often to my thoughts. An informed
public is a progressive public, said the editor this
month, concluding his editorial.

I took my typewriter outside and sat in the sun,
looking down on the lake, accompanied by Pretzel,

Mary's dachshund. She had two young Indian dogs playing with her, but although they towered over her she was very much Top Dog. I noticed that when children passed by on their way to the clinic they drew back from Pretzel, and hid behind their mothers' skirts if she came near. The mothers too drew back. Yet none showed any fear of the wolf-sized playmates, and Pretzel by white standards was an endearing little dog, and gentle. They called her "*kenaypik*," a generic, derogatory word that covers snakes and worms and slithery things. Cats were virtually non-existent in Sandy — the village dogs saw to that. Mary brought her Siamese but it was killed within a week or two.

When we had first come, the trees under which I was sitting were bare; now, the leaves were almost entirely unfolded. It was a perfect time in the North, that brief season immediately after *minookamin*, the break-up of ice, and just before the flies have realised that it's summer again, the wicked hordes of hungry black flies.

The sun beat down strongly in this pure clear air, and I fell asleep, awakened by the arrival of the weekly mail plane. I watched it taxi in to the Bay post, and soon I saw the factor and his assistant, and several other helpers, toting the boxes of groceries and freight and the sack of mail up the hill. Almost

Hair Styles

immediately afterwards, the engines of the Fisheries plane taking off from the other side disturbed me.

And yesterday there had been the Lands and Forests Otter, with the game warden, come to collect the seal records (the metal tags affixed to all fur-bearing animals) and question the returning trappers on caribou and moose sightings, or kills.

Things were becoming too hectic — three planes in two days. I abandoned the idea of sleep, and called on Susan in her shack-studio — she had lured a magnificently hawkfaced Grannie into her studio, a face so arresting that she was actually expending one of her largest canvases on her. There was a cluster of giggling, inarticulate relatives in one corner; a small boy stood behind her, watching every stroke of the brush; and, on the ground, a very small artist was covering a piece of paper with chalk strokes. She told me the latest news: the two-days-overdue Beardy canoe had arrived, Mary was marinating moose steaks for tonight, young Tullia Heron had eaten half a tube of cadmium yellow.

I spent the rest of the afternoon peacefully at the far lonely end of the rocky peninsula, grubbing around the lakeshore banks with a pen-knife and a trowel, for this must have been the site of another village long ago. I was rewarded with some pieces of pottery, but they were miserably small fragments and rattled sadly around in my packsack.

On the way back, I called in at the cabin where the game warden had set up an office for the day. He had a young man along, a university student, as assistant, who would be left in this area as an observer for the summer. He told us that last summer he earned his living picking up buffalo droppings for parasitic investigation. There are more stimulating ways of passing the time than waiting around for obliging buffaloes, he observed. We decided that he should write a book about his experience called, we thought, *Dung Days*.

Woodland caribou held the centre of interest this year, and I listened to a discussion on their grazing and migratory habits for a while. Someone, somewhere, was conducting an extensive research and longed for dedicated souls to parcel up whole stomach contents and dispatch them to him for analysis, but he was hampered, apparently, by lack of material. "He doesn't seem to understand how difficult it is," said the warden sadly. "What trapper is going to parcel up any stomach let alone a caribou's, in the middle of nowhere, then snowshoe off to the nearest post with it? He'd have to be out of his mind."

I left, promising to fill my pack should I happen to find any disembowelled caribou on the way back to the nursing station. The pilot of the warden's Otter went with me to show me his "little old dog,"

who accompanied him everywhere. He opened the
door to the rear and an enormous brown-white bulk
surged out and flowed down the steep ladder steps.
His little old dog looked like the offspring of a St.
Bernard and a Kodiak bear, and was apparently not
yet fully grown. We were recorded for posterity by
the lens of the aerial photography camera, our eyes
almost on a level.

We watched them come in on Treaty Day, tying
up their Beechcraft at the dock below the nursing
station: the agent, the welfare officer, and an assistant, who were to sleep in the Lands and Forests
shack down by the beach. By the time we got to the
R.C. school, where the treaty ceremony and paying-
out were to take place, tents and stalls were being
put up for the "concessions." (I.e., someone buys a
case of pop from the Bay and sells it on the conces-
sion for two cents more.) The flag slapped briskly
outside as the people filed past the agent and his assistant in the schoolroom. Ceremony, here as at Big
Trout, has dropped nowadays to nothing more than
a kind of catching-up on welfare records. "Good
morning, what's your number? How many kids?"
Long pauses while the real kids were separated
from the adopted ones, and the ones that were being
"looked after." This process took real patience on
the part of all, from Indian to interpreter to agent
and back again. Finally, the number was settled on

and verified in large ledgers, and a cheque was filled
out: $4.00 per head, as agreed in the Coronation
Scheme Treaty between His Majesty King George
and his Indian subjects here. His Majesty, I noted,
also agreed to provide suits of clothing for the chief
and counsellors, one of which Moses Kakapetum
was wearing — a navy blue reefer jacket with brass
buttons and "Counsellor" emblazoned on the side.
Sometimes there were complications — a band
member who had been defranchised and now
wished to return to the reserve, an illegitimate child
who was not yet officially born — as an exhaustive
hunt through the ledgers failed to produce him.

Unaware of his non-existence, young Master
Wawageesic gazed out tranquilly from the laced-up
cosy prison of his brightly embroidered appawasian.
He was referred to the welfare officer, along with
an old woman with a fine dark face who was claim-
ing old age pension but was unable to produce any
proof of the date of her birth. She insisted that
she was seventy. How old was she when she was
married? . . . . Thirteen. Where was she born?
. . . . Deer Lake. Her father's name, her mother's
name, the name of every child who survived a year.
When a great deal of information had been ex-
tracted, and after much adding and subtracting
of dates, it was found that either she was sixty,
or else there were ten missing years in her life. But

she persisted. She offered her brother as proof — he was two years older. And how old was he? "Seventy-two, of course," she said, amid gales of laughter from the audience of cronies awaiting their turn. "Were you baptised?" asked the agent in desperation. Yes, but she didn't know where. It might have been Deer Lake. "How old were you?" persisted the agent. Immense giggling. "I mean, can you remember your baptism?" This convulsed the audience for some reason, and the interpreter, laughing himself, refused to give the exact text of her reply.

Susan was sketching in the far corner, her pencil flying over sheet after sheet of paper, surrounded as always by a fascinated group. I sat as unobtrusively as possible near the welfare officer, nearly lulled to sleep at one point by the gentle creaking of wood against wood as a young girl moved the top of a propped-up cradleboard to and fro. The child was nearly white, and this time it was fortunate that it was illegitimate, for she wanted it to have Indian status and to be brought up within the band, which had raised no objection (although they were within their rights to do so). This would not be possible, and she herself would lose her band membership had she married a white husband; only the women are discriminated against this way, which is patently unfair. The welfare officer was filling out official forms, and it took a long, long time, during which the young girl sat utterly still, save for the gently rocking hand, her face devoid of expression. He gave her the forms to sign, and slowly and patiently explained what she was signing. "This is to say that you will have nothing more to do with him; this is to say that all you have said is true; this is to say . . ." She signed all trustingly, and without comment. I hope the day will soon come when our Indian Act is amended to right, among other archaic despotisms, such discrimination.

The steady file went on all morning, until they took a break at lunch-time, and, by late afternoon, everyone was ticketed, docketed, paid, and stamped with the Seal of Government Approval. Outside, on the meadow, there were more tents up, pop music was being relayed, and families sat on the grass in relaxed picnic groups. There may not have been the dressing up in brand-new store clothes as there was at Big Trout, but the clothes, as a whole, were far more colourful, and there was more of a festive community spirit. The Norval Morriseaus were quite sensational, he in his beaded buckskin, and Victoria, his wife, in gold lamé, while Norval, unusually for an Indian family, carried the tikkanagan, the cloth embroidered in a spectacularly beautiful design, which he told us was his own.

The sports in the evening brought a relaxed, amusing, almost family air. They were held in the field by the Hudson's Bay Post, and Marsh, the factor, was the master of ceremonies, aided by Barrie, the young Micmac schoolteacher. Mary ran a very successful ice cream stand (a real treat here that many had never tasted before) on the steps of the Hudson's Bay post, so that she could make use of its freezer, assisted by the clerk. As a spectacle, the site could not have been better, for at 6:30 P.M. the sunlight lay long and mellow over a now golden land, the field sloped down to a blue and tranquil lake. During the canoe race, standing on the dock, I looked up the slope, and silhouetted unforgettably against an azure arc of sky, spilling down the slope, was the whole colourful community, and in the still clear air laughter rippled in soft waves towards me when Barrie and the agent took a canoe into the race and ended up a very blown and redfaced last.

There was a fierce tug-of-war, and races for children of all ages, but the women's race was the most joy to watch, the reluctant, shy entrants kidnapped and pulled to their feet by Marsh and Barrie, then propelled to the starting line, so that eventually, after much pursuing, badinage and persuasion, ten stalwart giggling matrons were lined up waiting for the start, one moccasin for each being removed first and piled in a heap at the half-way mark. The matrons showed a surprising turn of speed for all their skirts and bulk. The one that I was most certain would not succeed, being built on the lines of a Mack truck, ran like a deer and flashed past the finishing post two lengths at least ahead of the rest of the field, while the young long-legged one that Susan was privately betting on collapsed in a giggling heap on the moccasin pile.

Later, pleasantly exhausted with laughter and sun and the stepped-up pace of today's living, most of the white community gathered at the post for coffee, and the general talk inevitably returned to the reserve, and in particular to the problems of water, and here in this clearest, most uncontaminated part of the world, to the problem of local contamination, a recent test having given sinister results. "And no wonder," said Peter Armour, "with those leaking outhouses and the carefree attitude towards garbage." "What about chemical toilets?" I asked, but they thought no. Pail-a-day type of sanitation, with a septic tank? Too impractical here, for there was a seepage problem with the clay soil. Fancy then strayed idly to the best way to solve the problem, and ranged from a fifty-holer on the beach by the fast-flowing Berens River, to the suggestion from Marsh, that finally broke up the meeting, that the cheapest method of all in the end would be to charter a plane and fly everyone out once a week to a different island.

The Treaty group departed and close on its heels

came the Norseman carrying the X-ray party. So, Mary would have a busy day. I could hear her now in the clinic, above the steady sobbing of a child with a face grossly distorted from an abscessed tooth, scolding the parents for not bringing him in yesterday, the regular "sked" day for flying out patients who needed medical or surgical treatment at the hospital. The parents said that they came to the station yesterday but, "There was no one here." "Naturally," said Mary in worried exasperation. How could she be here when they had seen her handing out ice cream over at the post? Why did they not say anything then? Blank looks. Now, because of some unguessed-at barrier of communication between the white conception of common sense and time, and the Indian lack of it, (but based sometimes on something so apparently elementary to us that we do not begin to realise what difficulties it presents, either in terms of comprehension or the overcoming of shyness) the following operation to get the child to Red Lake had to take place:

Father Dumont was contacted through Marsh at the Bay, and set out in search of Donald, the X-ray pilot. Donald reported back via the same way that by luck the Fish-Run plane had just landed on the other side of the peninsula, so now Willie the caretaker took out the boat in the howling wind and set off to contact the Fisheries pilot who agreed to take the child as an emergency. In the meantime, Mary had sent a telegram requesting permission to evacuate the child, but, while she was awaiting an answer, the Fisheries pilot sent Willie back to say that he must take off now as visibility was closing down.

Yet the child had had the abscess for two days and must have been in torment. To our sophisticated minds it seems absurd. The parents had been at the sports the night before, had spoken to Mary, not mentioning the child, and, having spoken to her, walked to the station to see if she was there. Surprise, surprise, she wasn't. Back they went and watched the tug-of-war and bought an ice cream from Mary. Reminded of little Moses' abscess by his surprising petulant refusal of the ice cream, they returned to the station. Surprise, surprise, she still wasn't there . . . So are the Indians labelled stupid or feckless very often; but, to a people whose contact with the outside world is almost nil in some cases, their horizons limited to the trapline or the fishing camp, it would not be too far-fetched to suppose that possibly these parents knew only that an ailing child should be brought to the nursing station, and that it was sufficient, with the magic of white people's cures, to take the child to the *place* of healing only. (I remember one intelligent old man asking about Ottawa, that place where he knew the Queen sent her representative, where laws were passed, and, on hearing a description of his capital city, it was quite obvious from his further questions that he related everything to Sandy Lake. The Parliament Building would be the Community Hall, a traffic rush would be two skiddoos within half a mile of one another on the frozen lake, the universities the school, and hospitals the nursing stations. And was the trapping good there this year, he wanted to know. Were there many portages up the river to Parliament?)

Whatever the temperature by day, by evening on the lake one needs winter clothes. One night we went out in Father Dumont's boat, and I was glad of my eiderdown-lined hunting jacket on top of a heavy sweater. Father wore his beret at a nautical angle in keeping with the occasion. His boat was his pride and joy. It was built by one of the Oblate Fathers who had been at Sandy some twelve years before, to his own design, and the design certainly had a fine catholic originality — something like a cross between a half-decked fish kettle and a miniature sea-going tug, while the lines were almost pure Noah's Ark. "You would like to go and look at the old graveyard up the river, yes?" he suggested, knowing our ghoulish predilections, and off we set, skirting the shore of this enormous empty lake, looking for the river, the broad and mighty majestic Severn flowing north to Hudson Bay. "I wonder where it is," said Father, taking out a pair of spectacles held together with adhesive tape, and peering around the endless expanse as though expecting to find a signpost with "To the River" on it, and we putt-putted gently on in search.

There was a winging of ducks overhead, sometimes small flocks, but mostly in pairs: pintails, mallards, teal, and some beautiful little buffleheads. There were both hooded and redbreasted mergansers, and around a reedy bank some twenty or thirty nighthawks were skimming over the water, wheeling and diving after insects in the evening sun. All around, the lake was black and still, the only movement our lazily curling wake, and so pure and clear was the air that I could trace the sweet nostalgic smell of young poplar from the land. By some Oblate miracle, we found the river, gliding down it as though in a timeless dream. I found it hard to believe that the world was round on such an evening. There was the feeling that we could glide on right over the horizon and into space. I know why people return to this wilderness of ancient land, for all its loneliness and hardship, the constant elemental battling, the bitter endless winters, the voracious mosquitoes of summer, why, once they have come under its spell, they are never again free of it — for there is a magic here like no other place I know in the world. It is as though one had found something that one had known long ago but did not realise was lost until suddenly aware of a beloved familiarity.

High up on the grassy slopes beyond the banks most of the summer camps were occupied. Smoke-houses were going: "First a single line of darkness / Then a denser, bluer vapour / Then a snow-white cloud unfolding / Like the treetops of the forest / Ever rising, rising, rising / Till it touched the top of heaven —" The smoke plumes swirled across a bend in the river before us, illuminated by the low westering sun to a glowing Turneresque mist, yet flanked by a depth of landscape that was pure peace-ful Corot, while the sky behind the black silhouette of treetops flamed wildly to colours that no brush has ever captured.

Families were gathered in the peace of evening before the cabins. Children stopped whatever they were doing and stood stockstill until we passed, typ-ically with toes turned in and hands to mouth. We waved, but only the very bold waved in return.

The cemetery had an interesting palisade of long poles with ribbons fluttering from the tops. I had hoped to see a large carved wooden loon lying on one of the graves (probably of someone who had be-longed to the Loon Totem group) that was there last year, but it was gone, and I was sad, and some-how ashamed for the culture of which I am a part, for it would not be taken by any Indian from here. Wild strawberries were flowering there, and white violets, and only we three living people, and a grey owl gliding low against the treeline, moved in the tranquil silence of that place until, almost theatrically, as though to bewail some terrible loss, a loon cried far down the hazy river.

At dinner a few nights later I was summonsed by Maida. The chief and counsellor wanted to see me, she said. It sounded ominous. I wondered what I had done and what my fate was to be. Susan promised as I went forth to see that my scalp was returned to my family.

They were waiting in the entrance hall. The chief had decided to speak through Moses. He wanted to know if I was writing about Sandy Lake, and if so, what. His face was unreadable, remote, and looking at him I was reminded of a sentence from Dunning's book: * "According to an informant, the Chief of the Sandy Lake Band was the most powerful conjuror around." "No," I said, honestly, for I do not consider a diary or a commonplace-book writing, and I told him what I had told him before, that I was trying to finish an article that had nothing whatsoever to do with Indians, or even Canada. He decided to ignore this, or else Moses had told him something else, for when he next spoke it was to the already determined effect that when I wrote about Sandy Lake it should

* Dunning, *Social and Economic Change Among the Northern Ojibwa.*

be accurate. I should not seek my information only from, or listen to, those who did not know, i.e., the white people, but find out from the people themselves.

I was astonished! This was what I had always wanted, but did the chief *really* think this ideal was attainable? That an outsider could gain their frank confidence? He was one optimistic conjuror. "If I were to write about Sandy," I told him guilefully, crossing my fingers and hoping he would not suddenly turn me into a toad, "this is what I would want to do, but it would not be possible, for I think the village people here are the same as the village people among whom I grew up. If a stranger of another race came into their midst and asked many questions of their beliefs and ways of life, they would consider it an impertinence. They would not show anger or disregard him, because like your people they are a courteous people, they would simply say that they did not know, or some might amuse themselves by agreeing with anything he said in order to get him on his way again as soon as possible." I said the gist of this very slowly so that Moses would translate sentence by sentence. When he had finished both their faces cracked into amusement, and they laughed like a couple of schoolboys. I felt we had each other's measure now, and, momentarily anyway, we were on the same wavelength. "There are many questions I would like to ask," I added, with what I hoped was a smile of sunny frankness, "but I do not want to seem rude and curious, and so I hear only the white man's explanations."

The upshot of it was that the chief promised that he would meet with me and answer any questions that I might put to him. We parted with firm and friendly handshakes all round, and I searched my mind for some pleasantry to say in his own language to cement the friendship, but my days with the Missionary Bishop had only succeeded in planting one personal phrase in it, "*papa pingwa* — he has a jolly face," which I found very useful when admiring babies. "*Okinagan*," I said, hopefully, to Moses, indicating the chief. "*Papa pingwa*," and, jolly as old Saint Nick himself at hearing this, the chief departed — while I returned, delighted at the opportunity that had been dropped into my lap, to dinner (roast caribou).

In the next few days there was so much to do — I don't know why people always say, "What on earth do you find to do with yourself in a place like that?" — so much to see. More and more birds were arriving, wild flowers popping up, more and more patterns falling into place. We managed to fly to Deer Lake, Favourable Lake, and North Spirit, and there was a party one night for the departing Northwest clerk, when Marsh skidded his Hammond organ

over the hill from the Bay post to the nursing station, and there was the happy day when a Provincial
policeman flew in — after an acrimonious interview
or two he departed with Arthur and several of the
controversial reels of film from the schoolhouse, and
soon afterwards, with much sound and fury, un-
mourned, Rudi packed his leotards forever and flew
off too. The Sandy Lakers, having wrung the last
ounce out of this event, now occupied their minds
with more seasonal activities: from the amount of
heady horseplay and scufflings, giggling and sounds
of nightly pursuit through the bush, it looked like
being a busy and fruitful time.

In the meantime, I prepared some questions for
the chief ranging from the rumoured exploitations
of orphans in some families to the reasons for the
elders preventing young people leaving the band to
make their way in the outside world; the apparently
superstitious refusal of some of the older people to
have their likeness captured on paper; his reaction to
Morriseau's breaking with tradition, portraying
legends, and revealing medewiwin practises such as
tent-shaking and the Feast of the Dog; the meaning
of some of the pennants tied to stakes behind tents.
Would he tell me how much conjuring was still
practised, how many shamans and what powers
they exerted (dared I ask if he had retired himself or
not?), etc.? What heaven it would be if they were

all answered according to my standards of intellectual honesty. Every day I expected the chief and Moses to appear at some inconvenient time, and I carefully memorized some appropriately chatty phrases in his honour.

But when at last he sent a message to say that he was coming to talk to me at the station, we were packed and listening for the engines of the outgoing plane. Either he had picked his time perfectly, or it was another of those baffling racial impasses over time. Moses came too, but I asked Maida to interpret, for she did a far more accurate job. I managed to get in my "*Naspich ne sikelasin wapumittan*" — I am glad to see thee — but had to abandon my carefully rehearsed weather-small-talk alternative (the wind bloweth, the sun shineth, or the snow falleth, etc.). In the short time we had, it became apparent that the chief and I were only too alike in our mental make-up, and it resolved into an unspoken battle of wills. I wanted the promised information, but he was cagey, and his answers were evasive. He, I soon found out, wanted to use me only as an instrument to air grievances in print. This I was perfectly willing to be, but as I pointed out, I would not be a very impartial or honest instrument if I did not explore the validity of the grievances from both sides, and there was hardly time to cover this ground *now*. Why had he not come before? I

received the same blank look that Mary got from the
parents of the sick child. In the end, scribbling fast
and furiously against time, I took down all his many
points, and he answered a few of my questions: the
elders did not try and prevent the young people leaving (rot, I thought); the old people would not be
sketched for they couldn't sit long enough (rubbish!
Indians can sit longer and stiller than anyone I
know); Morriseau — he shrugged his shoulders
indifferently. Morriseau was not one of them; let
him therefore do what he liked. Adopted children —
perhaps there may have been, conceivably, it was
just possible, there may have been a little remiss-
ness, during the time when he was not chief, but
certainly not any more (!). I heard a distant dron-
ing of aircraft engines. "Do you know that you are
described as being the most powerful conjuror
around here?" I asked. He laughed, with a kind of
derisive snort. "I have heard that it is written in a
book," he said. "There are people who will believe
anything. What do they think I use? They will say
that anything I carry around is strange (I think he
meant suspicious) such as these," and he dug in his
pocket and tossed its contents onto the bench between us: two or three nails, a pebble, a box of
matches, and a dry brown root. He laughed again,
presumably at the childish gullibility of some people, but his eyes were more bright and alert than I

had seen them when I picked the objects up one by
one and examined them. "That is *very* powerful, be
careful, ha-ha," he said, when I looked at the root,
his jollity tacked on as an afterthought. By lucky
chance, I recognised it as being the same as those
which one of the northern nurses brought back from
Little Grand Rapids for us to try. I don't know from
which plant it comes, but it is dried and chewed as a
kind of panacea for commonplace ills, such as a sore
throat or stomach upset, as well as being a pleasantly aromatic thirst quencher. I decided to go along
with him — there wasn't time to do anything else
(and long gone, alas, were my happy dreams of the
cosy chat on conjuring that I was hoping might lead
to a good sound recipe for hexing unpleasant people
or obstructive objects). So I laughed, "ha-ha," like
an echo too, and broke off a piece of root; and chew-
ing it I told the chief that it would be just too bad if
it turned me into a turtle or something, for then I
wouldn't be able to write about Sandy Lake. "Ha-ha-
ha," said the chief, laughing just the way it is written and looking, I like to think, a little baffled.

"Hurry, hurry!" shouted Mary down the base-
ment steps, "The plane's there and he can't wait —"
and we surged upstairs where I handed the astonished chief my heaviest packsack — which he
swiftly transferred to Moses while I as swiftly
thrust my typewriter into his now-empty hand. As

Moses was now in the lead and I had set off at a dead run after him, the chief had no option but to follow, carrying the infra-dig burden. I felt much better. But the chief was wilier than I thought; he arrived at the dock empty-handed, smiling smoothly, and a small boy came steaming along with the typewriter. Honours were even.

Nollie already had one passenger in the plane, an Indian woman returning from the hospital whom we had to deliver to Deer Lake. She spoke no English, so conversation was very limited; she seemed to be still in a complete daze. And thinking about it, as I watched her at Deer Lake — following her husband, with whom she had exchanged no word, carrying her own bundle down the dock to where his canoe was moored, to be transported across the lake to possibly a canvas and spruce bough tent — how could she not be dazed? What unknown terrors must there have been for her, catapulted out of this background into a world where nothing could have held any familiarity; nothing could have made recognisable sense. It had the stuff of which nightmares are made.

In her place we picked up a prospector who had been in the bush for six weeks, his pack weighty with samples. He looked like a cat who has been at the cream, but responded to no pumping, however subtle. The first thing he was going to do, he told us, after he had locked up his samples safely for the night, was head for the beer parlour, and he licked his lips in anticipation. We dropped him, hurrying thirstily up the dock, at Red Lake. Nollie had some business to do, so we sat in the sun on the dock, eating the quiche Lorraine that Mary had providently packed for just such an occasion. From where we sat Red Lake looked like a miniature Naples, with all sizes and conditions of aircraft moored off the docks instead of gondolas. At last we arrived at Sioux Lookout, and there, walking down the main street where at least three cars were passing, and there must have been about twenty visible people, we felt as hemmed-in as though we were in some frantic metropolis. And the thing we were most conscious of was how very *pale* everyone looked; like the dead young lady in "St. James Infirmary" they were all "So cold, so clean, so fair."

We got into the car for the long drive home. It felt stuffy and strange. The radio came on with the ignition. We had not heard any news or read any newspaper other than *Kitiwin* for a long time, and now the outside world came flooding in. We turned it off before its troubles engulfed us, and found that we had a flat tyre: there was no escaping them. We were outside once more.

6

Fort Severn, Casabonika
and Yelling Falls

THE LONG TUBE of yellow knitting is pinned on the wall now above my desk, along with Willy's bone-scraper. The third item there that is without price is a round beadwork plaque depicting a very strange caribou, with a lecherous purple popping eye, and four identical legs, all shaped like the trousered hind legs of a pantomime horse. I never look at it without thinking of Father Saigan, and one of the most memorable day's fishing I have ever had, thanks to the nurse who took me along with her in a Cessna piloted by Henry, John's brother-in-law. Father Saigan was the Oblate missionary at Fort Severn, that little lonely community on Hudson Bay, perched high on the perpendicular clay bank at the mouth of the Severn River. He had a church that could hold two hundred, and a flock of two families in the community of some one hundred and fifty souls. I think of him now, so small and slight in that bleak windswept land, his rectory a sparsely furnished hut of not much more than six by ten feet — for the old one had burned down — with little more than the bare necessities of life, and his generosity with what he had: the warmth of his hut and a cup of coffee; the offer of his boat to go fishing in, a knitted scarf (and already he was unwinding it from his neck), an extra rod and reel. . . . And when I unwittingly admired that delightfully primitive caribou, the only decoration on his walls apart from a last year's calendar, it was to see it immediately plucked down, dusted off, and laid in my hand. It had been designed and executed by one of his small parishioners; he would not hear of its return. I had enough sense to restrain my enthusiasm over the cannonball he had dug out of the river bank, and the beautiful ammonites from the estuary, otherwise I am quite certain they would be with the plaque on my wall now.

In the end we did not borrow his boat to go fishing. Instead Henry and I took off in the little Cessna and flew a few miles up the coast to where the estuary of the Pippiwatin River widened to the short stretch of blue open water that was the first sign of any break-up of the ice in the arctic seas. We flew low over the water, looking for an open stretch among the boulders and sandbars and floes of rotting ice. Henry could land that Cessna in a saucer of water if need be, and it is as well that he can, for that is just about what we did do. Five minutes after it was moored, I was wading through the shallow rapids, picking a perilous course over the glacier-rounded slippery boulders, the foaming icy water pulling strongly at my waders. The waders were by courtesy of the Hudson's Bay factor, and were so large that I had no idea in which direction the feet were pointing or whether I was even standing on them; they concertinaed downwards without an anchoring belt for the straps. I teetered precariously in the middle of the river, and cast downstream; the water boiled up into a flashing silver arc almost before the little red plug hit the surface, and the line tautened with such a forceful jerk that I nearly over-balanced and was only steadied, and finally anchored — like one of those rubber figures with weighted feet — by the water pouring over the tops of my boots. Now what to do? I obviously had a monster — but no landing net or gaff, and Henry was lost to sight around a bend of the river. Play it, reel it in gradually, yes — but into what? My hat, or the top of my commodious boots? I saw a gravel spit, table-top size, some fifty feet away and headed

for it, waddling desperately on the insteps of water-
logged boots, like a seal on flippers, reeling as I
went, towing my fish behind me, until at last I
reached the gravel haven for the final mighty effort.
My prize leaped and curvetted in the air, back-
tracked and pirouetted before me as I drew him
closer, until finally I had him on a foot of line just
off the submerged tip of the short metal rod. I swept
him onto the gravel, and then, mad with excitement,
I leaped squelchingly on him and clutched him to
my heaving bosom. One clunk on the head with a
stone and he was mine. I wanted to shout aloud and
dance on my spit, but was hobbled by the boots, and
set off cautiously for the shore with my trophy, four
and a half pounds of deep-bellied shining speckled
trout, and there I laid him reverently by a marking
boulder, and immediately set forth again, not even
caring that my legs were by now so cold that I could
have been walking on wooden pegs for all the feeling I had below the knees.

I made that precarious journey to and from my
gravel top and the shore seven times in an hour.
Two fish out-manoeuvred my spectacular tackling
technique at the end of the battle, for my island
seemed to be shrinking: from dining table size it
shrank through kitchen, coffee and bridge table size
until finally I was trying to land my catch on something about the size of a TV tray. It was not until I

saw Henry sprinting past on the shore that I realised what had happened: inland fishermen as we normally are, we had completely forgotten that these were tidal waters, and the Cessna was straining to take off across the rising river. I saw Henry wade out to it, then a few minutes later the Cessna took off like a mallard jumping from a small slough, turned in the most astonishingly steep bank above me, and headed back east. I was so exhilarated, so madly happy, so gloriously soakingly busy that it did not even occur to me to wonder where he had gone or when and how he would return: he could have abandoned me for all I cared.

A soft steady south wind blew, the rushing jubilant waters sang in their freedom to the melodic shifting of ice floes in the estuary; the long light was golden, turning that desolate forsaken land, flat to its endless treeless horizons under the great arc of northern sky, to a paradise, created, it seemed now, for me alone.

I felt drunk with living, and when I lifted my head once to a sound above that I felt rather than heard, it was not to the sound of a returning Cessna but to the strong slow beat of wings, of a Whistling Swan, so close above me in all its legendary grace and beauty that I felt covered by the great expanse of pure white wing; the mate followed, and slowly and steadily they beat upstream. They dipped their heads as they passed over me in turn, incurious, fearless, their eyes round and calm; and I, humble and grateful, bowed my own in return. I had gone into an enchanted land that afternoon. . . .

Of course Henry came back for me — and brought David, the seventeen-year-old clerk from the Bay post, and Marg, to try their luck as well, later ferrying us out in two trips. If we had lost the Cessna earlier on it would have been embarrassing, because of our carelessness, expensive and uncomfortable — perhaps two cold days and nights of being marooned there until a search plane could come from the base. But three months later, for the factor and the young clerk, a similar incident led to their deaths. They too were fishing on this same river, with two Indians, but had gone there in two boats which they beached on the river bank. When they returned the Bay boat was adrift, and the two white men jumped into the Indians' freight canoe to go after it. They tried to start the engine but there was no response; by now they were in midstream, being carried down fast to the mouth of the river, and too late they found that there were no paddles in the canoe. The horrified Indians, standing on the bank unable to do anything, watched the canoe being swept out into Hudson Bay, the factor still desperately pulling on the starting cord. They walked back to Severn, some eight miles only on the

map but an endless, terrible walk of yielding muskeg or clay in practise, every yard an effort. It was
pitch dark when they got back, and it was not until
the following day that search planes were able to
come. But by then it was too late. Many days later,
among the forming ice, the upturned canoe was
spotted off Winisk, over a hundred miles down the
coast. It can be an enchanting land — but a cruel
relentless one when man does not accord it the respect of constant vigilance.

On another occasion six of us took off in a Norseman to spend the day fishing at Yelling Falls. I can't
remember what the excuse was — perhaps to look
for canoes and supplies cached there the previous
fall, pick up trappers' cached pelts, a patient, or
some freight — whatever it was I always found it
was better not to enquire too closely, just so long as
I got there. We caught enough pickerel that day to
satisfy our enormous appetites on the spot, taking
turns in the canoe that someone had cached there
high on a platform among the spruce, one holding it
steady below the fast water from the rapids above
and two fishing — and hauling in for a period almost as fast as they could dispatch the fish and cast
again. There is nothing in the world like pickerel
cooked over an outdoor fire and eaten ten minutes
after it has been caught.

Later in the fresh golden afternoon I walked up

the portage trail and cast over the rapids, walking slowly along the bank to where the river was quiet and tranquil, and there I sat on the brilliant yellow lichen of a sunwarmed rock in the shallows, letting my line run idly downstream. Behind me on a rise of ground, sheltered from the prevailing wind, the spruce were unusually tall and healthy-looking, and there was a stand of beautiful jackpine. Warm and peaceful on my rock, lulled by the river sounds and the sighing of the wind through the jackpines — and some Calvinistic gene must needs suggest I make myself cold and energetic. There was a nice deep pool beyond my rock — and seconds later I jumped in: almost on the same impetus, like reversing a movie, I shot out again: the water was chilling to the very marrow of my bones. My teeth chattering like castanets still, I reeled my line in. There was a small jackfish on the end; I did not want it, but the hook was so imbedded that I had to kill it, and left it there on the rock with my rod and ran up the height of land to get warm. When I came back, so quietly and circumspectly, it was in time to see an otter in all its equally soundless but sinuous grace enter the water on the far bank, its sleek black head visible for a few yards when it surfaced upstream then finally dived again; and a huge black northern raven, Kakake, hopping and strutting over the rock to my jackfish. Just as it reached the prize I, most

selfishly in the circumstances, teased it with a rau-
cous "kark kark." The untidy black head swivelled
round, it saw me, and with indignant beady eyes it
took off. Unrepentant, I attached the fish to the end
of my hookless line again and retired to cover on the
river bank, thinking that I might tease him further
by twitching the fish over the rocks if he came back.
But the raven had his revenge, for in the peace and
quiet of the afternoon I fell asleep, and when I
awoke it was as though the fish had never been, for
not one trace remained of it, only the knotted line.
Perhaps Kakake, the cunning one, caused me to fall
asleep; I could believe anything here, for there is no
land like this, so clear and silent and yet filled with
the whisperings and movement and sound of those
who have their ancient life and being there, waiting
only for the intruder to leave so that they may re-
sume their form again. If one grows in stature here,
as I think everyone must, it is because one comes to
terms at last with one's human insignificance.

Flying back to Big Trout that evening, the cabin
redolent with the large box of pickerel at our feet,
we passed over a lake where two toy-like planes
were moored. Poachers probably, said John, the
pilot. It was impossible for this vast land to be properly patrolled, and therefore only too easy for them
to nip over the invisible border, landing in some remote water, where in some instances they even set

nets, before returning with a fine cargo of fish that would fetch a handsome price forty-eight hours later in some New York restaurant.

Later, ludicrously in all that emptiness, we spotted another small plane flying below us in the opposite direction. We altered course and climbed, John explaining grimly that there wasn't enough room in the whole world for that machine and his. It was no poacher this time, but an Evangelist Reverend, probably bound for a mission on a nearby settlement, though apparently heaven alone knew how he ever got anywhere, for he had a disconcerting habit of taking off and landing his "Wings of the Gospel" (the name was painted on) across wind. John told us how that winter, in forty-degrees-below-zero weather, he was at work on his faulty engine, but having difficulties as he lacked some type of spanner or ratchet. Just then the "Wings of the Gospel" — John had a far better though unprintable name for it — made one of its spectacular landings on the ice and came taxi-ing up to the shore, where the Reverend opened a window and inquired what was amiss. John explained, and asked if he had the necessary tool: "No," said the Reverend, and added unctuously that he never carried any tools — only "the Sword of the Lord." It was too much for the frozen, frustrated, oil-streaked John; in one short succinct phrase he told him what he

could do with it. Since then they had, by mutual
consent, avoided a further meeting.

That night we distributed pickerel all around,
and still had enough for a feast of the cheeks in the
nursing station. It was a most memorable day.

There was another day, equally memorable but in
a different way, when we managed a ride to Casabonika — a place we had particularly wanted to see,
the chief there being one of those who wished to lead
his people away from the corroding influence of the
encroaching world. So far he had succeeded in enclosing most of the village within a palisade, within
which in time he hoped to forbid the admission of
any white person other than the agent, except upon
the payment of a toll. We went there (with his consent of course) that morning and found it the most
unique and beautifully conceived plan — there were
twelve apostolic entrances in the palisades, and
within, narrow paths had been cut through tower-
ing spruce and jackpine, giving the effect of soaring
cathedral transepts; and in a silence filled only with
the wind soughing in the topmost branches, one
walked to the far end of a diagonal to the church,
now only in skeleton outline — a floor and the up-
standing two-by-fours, and incongruously on the
middle of the floor one very Gothic seat that would
have done credit to a bishop in any cathedral. The
cabins and dwelling places of the inhabitants were

scattered inconspicuously among the trees on either side of the walks. No dogs were allowed within the palisade, and all outhouses had to be erected without. Casabonika kindled one's hopes for a compromise, a resurgence of ideals and independence within the framework of common sense. The aesthetic aspect was interesting too, for generally it is something that no Indian considers.

We ate our lunch on the shore under the eyes of a silent group that seemed to be composed of most of the island's population, then Susan disappeared into the depths of a distant matagwan in company with an old moccasin-making friend, Rebeka, and two or three children carrying her painting gear. Alone, and unnerved by my silent audience, and the almost total lack of communication — when they did say anything it seemed to be a patois mixture of Cree and Ojib — and mindful of the meaning behind the creation of the palisade, I looked about for something unobtrusive to do; exploring around seemed to be out, too noseyparkerish; any hopes of advancing my vocabulary were obviously doomed too; I would look demented picking wild flowers, and furtive stalking birds — it looked as though I would have to spend the rest of the afternoon throwing stones in the lake, or asleep on the beach. At that moment Eno, the Free Trader's clerk, appeared, and I was inspired to ask him if there was any chance of some fishing. Without a word he went back into the store, took a rod off the wall, turned the key in the lock, and led the way to a freight canoe. Five minutes later we were putting gently along the lake, heading for the rapids where the river emptied into another lake. It was a brilliant fresh spring afternoon and it seemed that even as I looked, colour was surging back into the land. I felt very content and free. Sometimes we passed so close to shore that I could see splashes of colour along the interstices of the rocks, the blues and yellows of harebells, rock phlox and cinquefoil; and sometimes, brought to my notice only because of the canoe beached in front of it, a spruce- and spagnum-covered tent shelter, almost completely camouflaged, in the bush. Eno was a perfect companion; he entered into any project yet never uttered a word, only smiling when he understood what I wanted. He landed me on some rocks so that I could pick some specimens of the flowers to press in my notebook, and picked some sorrel and violets himself, delighted to find that I like to chew the leaves too; when I asked him to cut the engine so that we could drift as close as possible to a busy darting flock of nighthawks by the shore, he had the paddle out almost before I finished the sentence, and seemed as spellbound as I at the incredible aerobatics before us, the graceful forktailed forms wheeling as fast as the eye could follow (so that sometimes it seemed as

though we were seeing only an intricate fast-chang-
ing pattern of white patches against the dark background of the trees), and sometimes going into a
perfect nosedive. We were close enough to hear the
soft rushing noise of these dives, then the strange
little hollow boom just as the bird straightened out,
almost as though a miniature sound barrier had
been broken, making an effective drum accompani-
ment to the harsh high cries that Eno imitated so
perfectly. I could have stayed there the rest of the
afternoon, but eventually Eno started up the horrid
human effrontery of the engine and headed on for
the river. There, with the fine spray blowing on our
faces, we cut it again, Eno picking up a paddle, so
that the world was filled with the sound of fast-
running water surging and foaming cleanly over the
rounded boulders, with every now and then a small
perfect rainbow forming. Seemingly without effort,
Eno held the canoe upstream while I cast, but his
spinning reel had eccentricities all of its own and I
was not very successful, after many strikes landing
only one pickerel and then nearly falling overboard
in my excitement. After a while I suggested that he
have a turn and handed over the rod in exchange for
the paddle. With a deadpan face he gave it to me —
and three seconds later we were fifty yards away
from the rapids, while I, purple-faced with the
effort, every muscle shrieking in protest, was still

trying to turn the bow upstream. "Eno —" I shouted despairingly, my mind filled with lithographs of bearded voyageurs with woolly tams and rolling eyes bobbing by capsized canoes — wordlessly as ever he exchanged implements and the canoe leaped obediently through the swift water and back to the riffle below the rapids. Fishing in great humility after that, I caught three pickerel in succession. Curiously, Eno would not kill them for me, a job I hate doing, but only smiled gently and enigmatically, and handed me a spanner.

When we got back to Casabonika I tried to give him some money, but he shook his head and refused to take it, even when I explained it was my contribution towards the gas we had used. But he was adamant, and all I could persuade him to take was half the catch.

Back at the store, as there was still no sign of Susan or the returning plane, he taught me to count in Ojibwa. Sitting on the steps in the sun, with a pile of pebbles between us, we played shops. I would point back at something in the store, perhaps a saw, and ask how much, "*Einyminook?*" Eno would consider the saw very carefully, then give me a price, "*Ningotassah ahbik*," whereupon I would count out five pebble dollars: "*Neesin, nissin, naywin, neeanin*, NINGOTASSAH." Soon, by adding something that sounded like g-zapp for the teens, I was able to buy more expensive items like traps and boots. By the time Susan had returned I was up in the hundreds bracket, squandering my pebbles on outboard engines and drums of oil. The last item that Eno sold his pupil was a little girl of about four, playing below us with an axe almost as big as herself: she went for seventy-five dollars — *with* the axe, he added gravely.

I think of my patient fishing companion and teacher now with much respectful affection. I learned a lot that day.

7

Ohnemoos: the Indian Dog

OHNEMOOS is Ojibwan for Dog; if there is more than one dog it becomes Ohnemoosuk. And there always *is* more than one Indian dog: there is, in fact, a great unwanted surplus of Ohnemoosuk around every settlement, but nowhere is one more conscious of this than on Post Island. In spring when the ice is newly gone out, the ranks of the already undernourished canine population are swelled by the dogs that have followed families back across the ice from the winter's traplines on the mainland, and are now marooned on this small barren island. One can no more escape their presence than they can escape themselves; they cannot even merge into the usual village background of dense spruce forest, for here there are only small scrubby trees rising from the muskeg on the low uninhabited side of the island.

It is the rare dog who will depart again before freeze-up; who is valued enough to take up space in a family canoe, and reach the canine paradise of the summer fishing camps, there to gorge on fish guts, suckers and *mesea*. Perhaps the family dog to guard the camp, or scare bears off the women and children's blueberry patches while the men are out fishing; perhaps there might be room for a child's puppy. Until recently one would almost certainly have seen some sled dogs crammed in with the pots and tents, provisions, nets, and babies laced into carrying boards and propped against a thwart, but the mechanized sleds, the Bombardiers and Snocats, have almost replaced these. Poor Dog, poor Ohnemoos, is just another mouth to fill in a harsh country, and as such to be disregarded by the Indian, who often has a hard enough job filling his children's mouths. Thus Dog is back almost where he started in his relationship with nomadic Man, one of a ring of hopeful jackals or wolves circling the seasonal camps, already convincing himself that some benefit must stem from an association with Man. He must fight for his own existence, starve or survive, the inexorable rule of Nature that has governed man's own evolvement here, and which prevails still

in the attitude of the Indian to Ohnemoos today:
Nature is of necessity pitiless.

Because it is always spring when I think of Post
Island, Ohnemoos is howling — from primeval
longing perhaps, a hymn of the lengthening days,
the burgeoning of ancient smells in the thawing
muskeg; but above all he howls from hunger, for it
is the leanest time of his eternally lean year. The
haunting melody of his Spring Song rises and falls,
the cadences picked up by dog after dog across the
island until the great final crescendo echoes from
shore to shore and dies at last in mournful waves far
out on the imprisoning water. He laments, most bitterly, the small game that has long since gone from
the island, the last plump cat; he bemoans the ad-
vantage of the scavenging gulls with their wings;
and he bewails the unsatisfying qualities of mollusc
and root, the unyielding refuse dumps. His song is
the background music of the North, and, like the
sound of wild geese, never entirely leaves the heart
of one who has once heard it.

Children and puppies go together. The Indians
adore and indulge their children, so there are often
accepted woolly puppies tumbling around in the
mud or dust outside the cabins and tents along with
sloe-eyed toddlers, but when the pup grows unat-
tractively lean and gangling, overtaxing the already
meagre household scraps for house and sled dog, it

will be driven out to join the ownerless chorus that roams the village and surrounding thin bush. Round and round the island they go, wraithlike, through stunted trees, sniffing along the shore, trotting the paths between the low shrubs of Labrador tea and juniper, sunning and squabbling among the white cribbed graves in the churchyard. They lurk warily, a weather eye cocked for the stinging stone, around the Indian dwellings, drooling over the savoury redolence of beaver or sturgeon's roe smoking — safely — over a slow fire; and ingratiatingly outside the white picket fences of trading post and nursing station, schoolhouse or rectory. Here lives the White Man, and the canine word has gone around that he is notoriously wasteful with his potato peelings and eggshells, his bits of gristle, burned toast or apple cores. Besides, almost everyone feeds at least one extra waif along with his own dog: today might be the very day he will take on two . . . Round and round the island they go, ever hopeful that the next round will produce some minor miracle — perhaps a beaver pelt, scraped clean and stretched to dry on a frame, will blow down from a roof's safe-keeping; perhaps a snowshoe, with some tasty moosehide thonging, a moccasin stitched with nourishing deer sinew, from a platform cache; perhaps, with any luck, since the last visit, there will be a chocolate-smeared child's face to lick, a fishbone here, a fledgling there. And whatever it might be, the lean snarling bitches with litters will almost certainly pounce on it first, so round and round they go again. And I, exploring the island, on my own rounds, soon came to recognise each one of the pack: thin, often mangy or lame, fiercely cringing, warily aggressive, sneaky-eyed, for the most part unlovely pariahs.

Or so I thought at first, shocked and unhappy, fresh from a society that must pay for the privilege of owning a dog, and is liable for prosecution for its neglect. But when I came to know them better, Ohnemoosuk of Post Island taught me a very different lesson: ragged and gaunt they might be, an S.P.C.A. nightmare, but they had an unquenchable spirit and ebullience. One day, watching a mangy half-grown pup drag up an old fishing net from the sand and tear off along the beach with the whole sorry pack in high delight after him in a glorious tumbling game of tag, I realized that we do Dog an anthropomorphistic injustice when we link him with terms of pathos and maudlin sentiment: Dog is an incurable optimist, whatever his circumstances.

When one had realised this and could be objective about them, island confinement provided an ideal study in a form of Darwinism; although I could never make up my mind whether it was the fit or the witty that survived there, for I have never encountered so many unforgettable personalities among so many scrawny dogs. After a while I even began to believe that I was witnessing what I can only describe as a rehash of evolution: Ohnemoos was developing an interesting new line of ingratiation towards provident visitors.

Pepra was a good example of this evolved super-scrounger, and the one I came to know the best. Thin as a greyhound, blonde and leggy, with artful wolf eyes that could take on a professionally abashed expression calculated to melt the stoniest heart, she looked as though she had not had a square meal since the day she was weaned. Theoretically she was not ownerless, belonging to one Susannah, a somewhat flighty character who had other things on her mind — such as an assortment of children and no husband — and little therefore to spare for a dog. Pepra must have had me marked down from the moment I stepped out of the Cessna onto the dock, for she came begging round the door of our shack almost before I had unrolled a sleeping bag, and soon established herself as the top-dog cleaner-upper after meals. I encouraged her, for her very obvious attempts to charm amused me; then one cold evening I made the fatal mistake of allowing her to push her way in for a warm by the stove, after which she became extremely possessive. No sooner had she established her status than she dealt

briskly and forcibly with any other beggars at the
door. She is bound up inextricably with memory of
Post Island, for Pepra was not going to lose sight of
her meal ticket for one minute if she could help it.
Every inch that I explored of the island was in her
company; and as she seemed to have innumerable
friends and relations among the other roaming,
hunger-restless dogs, they usually tagged along too.
After a while I became resigned to the fact that if I
wanted to go and search for fossils or flowers or artifacts, every stone that I turned over, every plant,
was going to be examined by my interested following as well.

They were a raggle-taggle train for the most part,
often snarling and fighting among themselves over
some morsel picked up on the way. At first if their
quarrels took place too close for my comfort (I am
unreasonably terrified of the noise of dog fights), all
I had to do was pick up a stick or stone, brandish it
threateningly, and all would cringe off with flat-
tened ears and lowered tails — a parody of servility,
for their eyes reminded bright and watchful. They
were either very intelligent or very anxious to please,
for in a remarkably short time quarrelling was confined to a tolerable distance: I could almost see them
measuring the ground between us out of the corner
of an eye before setting to. They seemed to be only
token demonstrations, all teeth and noise and little

else. After a while all I had to do was say "psssss," a
noise I found no dog could stand, and order was instantly restored.

Having no option, I spent many hours observ-
ing the individual and pack reactions. Pepra had
developed a fascinating technique that some of the
small dogs were just beginning to adapt for themselves: she would collapse on her back at the first
warning snarl over some tidbit, the traditional
surrendering, but taking care to collapse her hips
on the morsel. Meek and apologetic, she would
lie there, tail tip quivering placatingly, while tradition now demanded the victor step back stiffly to her
acknowledgment of defeat; then, quick as lightning,
she would stretch her head backward along the
ground, swivelling her hips while at the same time
the middle of her body was righting itself — and
before the other dog had time to grasp the meaning
of this U-bend wriggle, she would be off with the
morsel, fast as the ludicrous shaggy greyhound she
resembled.

There were two pups in the pack that interested
me particularly as a study in contrast. They were
very alike in colouring and height, and the shape of
their heads, and may well have been litter brothers,
but while one was plump and jolly, the other was
very thin and nervous. The plump and jolly one I
knew was regularly fed at the nursing station, and

only came along for the fun: he was the good-na-
tured butt of the rest of the party, being forever
jumped on, rolled over or buffeted. The other was a
sickly, irritable little thing, with little energy, forever sitting down to scratch. One day he sat down
near me to have a prolonged session with his fleas,
and I noticed that he had a rope collar on. It was
already straining cruelly around his growing neck,
so I cut it off. Where the woolly fur had been chafed
away on his throat there was a raw crescent of skin.
He was such a poor little runt that I could not over-
come the eternal (white man's) urge to be a do-
gooder: I had a tube of calamine ointment in my
pocket that I always carried around to stop me
scratching mosquito bites, and I applied some of
this to the raw throat. I should have known better.
Within seconds he had disappeared entirely from
view under a scrimmage of excited dogs. Whether it
was the calamine or the base it was obviously a canine delicacy. When the pup eventually emerged he
had been licked clean and his throat was twice as
raw from the rasping tongues. And before I had
time to put my glove back on, I thought my oint-
ment-smeared fingers were going to be sucked into
the avid mouth of Walleye Junior, an unprepossess-
ing character who looked like a small motheaten
wolf. I never interfered again.

Walleye Junior and Walleye Senior were another

interesting couple who used to join us from the other end of the island. Senior was one of the oldest and most indomitable dogs, with half of his left ear missing, two toes on his left front paw, and almost all the hair from his left flank. I used to try and imagine what possible combination of circumstances had brought about these losses. He was a surly dog, which was hardly surprising. He and Junior made an eerie picture together; about the same height, they always ran with the opaque white eyes between them, so that one got the strangest impression of a kind of dual three-eared head with a pair of tinted glasses on the inner eyes, and an outer pair of sharp upward-slanted eyes enclosing them. Of course I tried to convince myself that they stayed together as an arrangement of mutual benefit, but common sense tells me now that it is more likely that the blind eyes were congenital, and that the pair were probably siblings and had always naturally run together. At the time I was watching them I was so engrossed in an atmosphere of the fiercest determination for survival that I would have believed anything.

Sometimes I returned to the shack after one of these afternoon's expeditions along the trail that passed close to the fenced-in-compound of the weather station. There, in safe and solitary glory, sat the only pedigreed dog on the island, a Springer spaniel: from his smooth domed head with the long marcelled ears to his frilly leggings and gleaming Fauntleroy shirtfront, he was immaculate. And as exotic there as the Little Lord himself in the northern bush. My scaramouche friends gazed through the fence in silent awe; there were never any rude scufflings or derisive barks; Ohnemoos knew his place apparently (although I must admit I wondered if he would have retained it, and what he would have done to those ears, if the fence had not been there —). Lord Springer in return gazed through and beyond the hungry peasants at his gate. I thought he looked infinitely bored and rather stupid. At the end of two weeks I had added "effete" into the bargain and felt positively sorry for him. Given the choice, I would rather have been even old Walleye any day.

I was at once fascinated and strangely moved by my following's reaction to me over the time I spent with them. Apart from Pepra there was no association with food, for after the ointment episode I never so much as carried even a piece of chocolate with me: I had seen how easily one might become a rather battered bone of contention. And, apart from that, they were too many; anything left over to share after Pepra had been around would have been a useless drop in the bottomless maw of their hunger. They got nothing from me except my remote and somewhat schoolmarmish presence. They came only because of their strange, age-old craving for man's company. I began to understand why the Ojibwa had placed them uniquely somewhere between man and spirit animal in the mythology evolved count-less centuries ago.

Ohnemoosuk of Post Island led a most wretched bare existence by any standards, yet the overall im-pression was that they were not turned mean by it; they were in no way savage. The sceptic might say that they were too weak from general malnutrition to be savage, and to that I can only point out that any excess energy I saw was spent in chasing one another in play. Yet, less than a hundred miles away in another Ojibwa settlement, Ohnemoos of Fort Severn gave a very different impression.

One day, lured by the prospect of fossils to be found on the river bed at low tide, I was lucky enough to be offered a ride in a Cessna bound for Severn. Flying due north, we saw the dark conifer-ous belt gradually thinned out to barren treeless land — at one point so desolate in its conformation of wave-like ridges with the long-drawn-out gleam of water in their hollows that it looked as though the world was an endless empty shore waiting for the turn of some global tide gone out at the beginning of time. The horizon seems so round, the earth so flat there, that Hudson Bay was not visible where it merged with the tundra until we were almost upon it — bleak, grey-blue ice stretching to meet the grey-blue sky, with a thin line of vividly blue water marking the shoreline.

The small scattering of buildings that is Fort Severn huddles low to the ground, backs turned to the north wind, and safely away from the eroding clay precipices that line the mighty Severn's last sweep into the Bay. The Cessna landed in midstream, then taxied in until the floats rested against the landing at the bottom of a forty-foot clay bank. As I climbed out on to the slippery treacherous clay, two small balls of fur detached themselves from the carcass of a gull and went for my boots; getting a firm grip on the lace-holes, they started worrying them like the gull, so that I lost my balance and nearly fell in. They clung like furry limpets until the Indian who was holding the wing kicked them, whereupon they fell upon one another. One was snow-white, with long guard hairs, like a polar bear cub, and the other was its chocolate-coloured brother — both with the most savage demoniacal little faces I have ever seen on puppies, without one trace of the milk-blue innocence one usually finds in the eyes of anything so young. I met them again later at the factor's: they were now fighting for possession over what I thought was a bone, but on closer examination turned out to be a dog's foreleg.

Probably Mum's, I thought — it would be in keeping with their characters if they had polished her off when she weaned them. . . .

They were my introduction to the dogs of Fort Severn: better looking than their brothers of Post Island in that they were bigger, with more husky in them than Indian dog, but the fiercest dogs that I have ever come across. There was not one answering spark of canine good feeling in their cold eyes when they lit on anyone who was not their owner, only a salivating appraisal of mobile meaty bones. The largest, the sled dogs, which were still plentiful here, were — thank heaven — staked out, their eyes wicked, their teeth bare as one passed by. Those wandering along the river path were thin and small, of the type that slinks off with raised lip when threatened, then creeps up stealthily behind with teeth at the ready for unwary heels. Plainly the smell of a white person was anathema to the lot of them. For the first time in my life I felt uneasy — to put it mildly — among dogs. How could I have called Walleye Senior a surly untrustworthy old brute? He was a veritable Nana compared to this lot: I would not have trusted one further than I could kick it — and then with armour-plated boots.

Fortunately my faith in canine nature at Fort Severn was restored by one half-grown pup. I was on my way to the shore and had stopped by at Father

Saigan's little cabin to borrow his rubber boots, and find out where the biggest and best fossils were to be found. As we were looking at his own beautiful specimens piled outside the door the pup crawled out from a refuge deep in a pile of logs, and joined us: to my surprise I saw for the first — and only — time a tail that actually wagged at the sight of me. He was a most engaging character, an indeterminate fawn and brown, the thick woolly coat making him seem quite substantial — until one patted it and felt the ribs sharp beneath — with one amber and one greenish-blue eye in a pointed intelligent little face. His unusual friendliness was soon explained: the kindly little priest had been feeding him the scraps from what must have been his own very meagre larder: it had been six months since the supply boat, and another two would pass before it could return through the ice of Hudson Bay.

I set off along the path that gradually sloped down towards the river, a dirty walk in clay that soon became ankle-deep. Looking back, only a few minutes later, I saw the pup tearing along behind, silhouetted against the sky on the high bank. He arrived at my feet in one long glorious slither, then ran on to take the lead. I was delighted to have such enthusiastic company. It was an enchanting day, with a soft spring wind blowing, and at last a mile or so of beach in tidewashed smoothness, marred only now by my Father Saigan footprints and those of the running, leaping, spring-mad puppy. The brown tundra landscape was desolate, Dali-esque, with house-sized slabs of greying ice piled haphazardly on top of one another at the edge of the tidal limits, as though giant children had been playing there with building blocks; and all the time a background of noise, rumblings and growlings, grindings and sighings, as huge chunks crumbled and fell. My heart was in my mouth several times when the pup climbed up the rotten ice, jumping from block to block after gulls; but he must have been an old hand at the game, for always he leaped to safety just before a segment roared apart.

We walked on, and soon the settlement was far behind, and there was just the pup and myself in the whole world, walking, it seemed, nearly at its rim — two infinitesimal figures in the vast primeval emptiness. Because these terrestial proportions so diminished us, because the pup was reduced to the whole proportionate measure of my normal circumscribed world, it was as though I saw every detail of him immensely magnified and clear: the fleeting lights in his tawny and blue-green eyes, every responsive quiver to the wind in the curved side slits of nostrils, each individual whisker antenna above his eyebrows, beneath his chin, standing out singly, even the separate action of his claws in the sand. I can see them yet in a clear timeless photograph taken by the heightened perception that was my mind's eye that day. He chased sandpipers that rose in a wheeling group only to settle again further on, he rushed barking to the water's edge whenever an arctic tern broke off from its watchful circling and plummeted down to the water, he dug for digging's sake as I turned over occasional smooth glacial boulders in my fossil quest. His enthusiasm so infected me at one point that I ran too; and my enthusiasm then infected him in turn so that he leaped at me and grabbed the canvas shoulder bag and made off along the edge of the water, my precious bits and pieces of specimens scattering as he went. It didn't matter; nothing mattered on a magic day like this. The fossils had been there for a million years or more: they could wait another million before I returned to pick them up.

Sometimes we looked up to the quick winging of paired ducks, and once to the slower majestic beat of Canada geese, flying so low that I could see the workings of the pinion feathers and the two neat contrasting lines that were the feet, tucked demurely into the snowy rump. They seemed to awe the pup as much as they did me — as he gazed up in wonder the strap of the satchel dropped from his mouth and I was able to retrieve it at last.

We turned when the tide came flooding back, for

I had no wish to be caught leaping not so lightly on the piled-up ice blocks. I returned to Post Island that evening with no fossils, no specimens of anything, but with the most vivid and exhilarating memory of an afternoon spent with a strange vagrant dog, part husky, part wolf, part Indian dog, who had thrown in his lot with a stranger human for a day. He followed me down the steep slithery ramp to the Cessna, when the land was washed by the mellow glow of the late northern sunlight, turning his eyes to mismatched topaz, and bathing him in the short golden glory by which I shall always remember him.

And I wondered for the hundredth time as we flew back, what quirk of evolution thousands upon thousands of years ago impelled Dog, alone of all the animals in the world, to throw in his lot with Man — even as this pup had done this afternoon. He had no evolutionary need of man either: as his cousins wolf and jackal can still testify, he could get along perfectly well without him. Deliberately, uniquely, he chose his lot. The enigma fascinates me.

Pepra was waiting for me on the dock: protesting her undying love and admiration, she indicated that she had spent a hungry day. . . . I taught her that evening to bark "please" and offer a paw for the reward of food. She learned both within about ten minutes. By the time I left Post Island she was greeting me with her new repertoire on every possible occasion, and I felt that her future subsistence was assured at the hands of all visitors to the island: Only a heart of solid stone will be able to resist the frantic message of that disarming paw.

8

Postscript

I T HAS NOT been my place in this book to pontif-
icate on the "Indian Situation" in Canada, only
to remark on people and places as I have found
them, from a very small, confined and individual
point of view. And if most of the people I have written about seem pleasant and endearing, it is because
I have found them that way. I admit quite freely that
I am biased.

Soon more and more people will be able to make
their own judgments. In the six or seven years that
have passed since Susan and I first stayed in the
schoolmaster's house at Lake Nipigon, many
changes have taken place in the public awareness of

the Indian people and their situation in a just Canadian society; the voice of the Indian is heard as it
has never been heard before by white people, not
since it faded into the outer silence of the reserves,
and most important, now it is listened to. The Indian Act will soon be amended, according to the
wishes of the Indian people. Once I saw only place
names and shacks at the Lakehead as a reminder of
them, but now, passing through the city at the times
of day when students are going to or returning from
school, I see many young Indians among them, and
an ever-increasing number from the far northern reserves. Instead of going to segregated residential
schools, often hundreds of miles away, they still go
hundreds of miles — but now live with families in
the city to attend the local high school.

I thought of them one day quite recently, sitting in
the schoolroom in a very small and isolated community, a background very similar to that from which
many of these youngsters had come.

I had been driven in by the cold, and sat down
at one of the desks pushed back against the wall,
for there was a clinic in progress. I looked around:
it was like any other one-roomed schoolhouse on
a reserve, with cut-out pictures from magazines
pinned on the wall, a brightly coloured alphabetic
mural, a cylindrical wood stove. On the blackboard
three straggling lines of variously crippled letters

told a sorry story: "Albert Duck is a noisey little boy; Happle Meekis must learn to bave himself; Semolia must learn to work Faster." On the wall beside my desk was a large simple poster depicting an eighteen-inch red toothbrush and a nice fat and tidy tube of toothpaste with a curl of pink paste issuing from it. Large black letters proclaimed WE MUST BRUSH OUR TEETH AFTER EVERY MEAL. I asked the nineteen-year-old schoolteacher what hopes he had of such a dictum being carried out in this very poor community, where the average family would consider anything other than food, equipment or clothes a scandalous outlay of money. He had no hopes at all, he admitted, but he was so appalled at the state of the children's teeth that he had instituted toothbrush drill at the school. He opened a cupboard and there was a row of some twenty labelled toothbrushes hanging from nails, and a large tin of tooth powder. He had bought the toothbrushes himself, but was finding the upkeep of tubes of paste for twenty enthusiastic little brushers twice a day too much for his budget, until fortunately he had come across a recipe for powder in an old book on cookery and household hints.

He was very fond of the children, and they obviously liked him in turn, but sometimes, he said, he despaired of leaving any imprint, any improvement, having been defeated only too often by the passive resistance put up by the parents, and his knowledge that, from the moment the children stepped back over the threshold of their homes, they were frequently adjured to forget the rules, golden or otherwise, that were taught in the white man's school. He knew too that if he pushed too far, perhaps about work, or truancy, it only made things more difficult for the child caught in the conflict of authority. He had two exceptionally intelligent pupils whom he had tried to persuade the parents to send out to residential school, where they would receive an education enabling them to be trained for a responsible position in life. Reasoning with them that it is this generation that must start taking on the responsibilities of their own people in their internal affairs, he quoted the changes that were taking place "outside." But in a land far removed from the medium of mass communication, "outside" could be outer space for all it meant to the parents. The answer of one father had been to remove his twelve-year-old son forthwith from school and take him on the trapline, and a flat "no" came from the parents of the other, a girl — she was needed at home, even if she did have three other sisters.

He despaired too of the educational materials he had to work with, the standard reading books for white children. They contained little of any recognisable import to these children. I looked inside one

and there was "Father" skipping, his briefcase on the
ground, and Mother standing by with a plate of
buns — presumably as a reward: "Jump, Father,
jump!" exhorted his children, one of them, inexpli-
cably, standing on its head. It was small wonder that
the parents dug their heels in if their children were
going to be exposed to such curious and unseemly
goings on "outside," said the teacher bitterly. And
why did the entire population have to be represented
by this insipid, unreal family who never apparently
went anywhere beyond some regional suburbia except on a Visit to the Zoo, the Circus, or Uncle
John's Farm? Why not here, or to an Eskimo settlement for at least an enlightening start? The history
books he showed me contained little of Indians
except their ultimate defeat and submission (and
one could not help getting the impression that those
who resisted the invasion of their territory had done
so in a very ungentlemanly way; first they "rose"
and then they "massacred," whereas the invaders,
having failed to "quell" these uncouth risers, thereafter merely "subdued" them). There were many
and lengthy accounts of the first great explorers and
voyageurs — every man jack of whom, as the young
teacher pointed out, would have perished without
the endurance and skill of those anonymous people
who not only guided them but taught them how to
survive, without the courtesy, help, and hospitality

from the many unmentioned tribes encountered on the way. He would like to see such history books re-written, with an opening chapter properly devoted to the ancient life and culture of the people whose land was to become Canada, a chapter that would not only make Indian children proud of their heri-tage, but enlarge the horizons of all others as well.

The young teacher had taken this year off from University, where he was studying to be an archi-tect. So far there had been no word of anyone to take his place, for it is difficult to find teachers willing to endure the months of separation and loneliness, and once again the schoolhouse would be closed.

In the meantime, there were the other children to think about, those who had made it "outside" and were theoretically on the way to a successful inte-gration between both worlds. It will not be easy for them, and much of the difficulty will lie in the de-mands of their own people upon them. The criterion of success in the white world is financial — the indi-vidual acquisition of property or dollars; but should an Indian too close to his own people achieve such success through a good job, he will be lucky if he can hang on to it. As I learned one day from Johnny Anishanabe, there is sometimes another side to their frequently quoted reputation for not sticking to a job. Anishanabe means "human being," but is usu-ally translated by us as "Indian," and Johnny was the popular white conception of the shiftless Indian; he lived in a shabby log shack with innumerable outbuildings leaning every which way and weeds pushing up through scattered trash, with many children and a slatternly wife whom I had at first taken for his mother; and he could never be relied on to stay at anything lucrative for long, doing odd jobs when the fancy apparently took him and collecting welfare the rest of the time. He was a most bright, intelligent and cheerful man, his children among the happiest I have ever met. One day I asked him during one of those jobless times, why he didn't sign up for one of the government manpower training schemes, where he would be paid while being trained; he had the requisite schooling to be trained as a heavy equipment operator. His answer was very revealing, and unexpectedly straightforward for an Indian: if he *did* earn good money, most of his wife's relatives, and a good many of his own, would immediately move in to help him spend it. In which case he wouldn't want to be the only one leaving for work each day while everyone was partying at his home, just so that they could stay to go on partying. . . . But why on earth wouldn't he just tell them to shove off and party elsewhere, I asked. He was quite shocked at this; apparently it would be a very improper suggestion among relatives: they expected to share, and they would have expected him to do the same had the position been reversed.

It was obvious that the once necessary tradition, that all should share in the kill so that the band could survive, was dying hard. This translation into modern parasitism must have a killing effect on ambition; for the first time I appreciated the double difficulties of forging ahead too quickly.

The Indian returning to his reserve in any public capacity has a hard time too. Or if he is ambitious, and is taken on, perhaps, as a clerk in the Hudson's Bay post, his friends and relatives will then assume that they are entitled to unlimited tick. Should he refuse them this, as he must, he will be slighted and maligned, and it will be a lonely life — neither fish nor flesh nor good red herring — that he will lead if he continues in his job. One man that I met, returning to his people in the capacity of public health assistant in a community that had no nursing station, had only been able to stand his frustration for six months. It was an uphill struggle enforcing hygiene and sanitation, but his defeat came with his prophylactic attempt to control the beginnings of an influenza epidemic: he summoned everyone to his house (another bone of contention, for by virtue of his post it was one room larger than anyone else's) to learn how to gargle. After the lesson, he assured them, free bottles of antiseptic would be handed out, and all temperatures taken twice daily. Most painstakingly he explained all the reasons for his actions, and in addition how a thermometer worked to help diagnose a fever. Not a soul turned up. The local medicine man, sulking because of a recent hint that his leaking outhouse was a menace to public health, had circulated his decree that the bottles of gargle were Very Bad Medicine indeed, stealthily calculated to cause sterility and impotence, and that a thermometer was actually a kind of glass lie-detector that would instantly show if the gargle had indeed been gargled or emptied out — in which case far more sinister and cunning methods would be brought into force. The people, he stated, would do far better to stick to the good old ways and try something from his personal pharmacopoeia of charms, roots and herbs ("or else . . ." one imagined him finishing suavely). No one wants to be on the wrong side of a shaman: the people meekly took out insurance against future health as well by purchasing cures and keep-offs from this astute man of business.

The voices of most of the Indian spokesmen emanate from the sophisticated bands in the East, and hardly penetrate to the northern bands. The very remoteness that has preserved their dignity is making it hard for them to catch up even with their own people in these fast-moving times. I attended one of the five Round Table Conferences held across Canada with representatives of the regional bands and representatives from Ottawa. The amendment to the Indian Act was the subject under discussion, all of the objectives of the government being outlined, along with an abstract of the thirty-four questions pertaining to the proposed new act. The representatives were supposed to have discussed these with their counsellors and people beforehand, and had the power to say yes or no on their behalf. Its language was as clear and simple as possible, the handbook attractively produced, and obviously someone had put a good deal of thought and effort into it.

Yet I, whose business is with words, often found it difficult to obtain a clear picture, and it particularly saddened me to see many of the people from the northern bands that I knew being very often puzzled too. Yet it was their future that was being decided, and history was being made. The contrast between the intelligent, knowledgeable approach — and by knowledgeable I mean a knowledge of government machinery and legislation — of the worldly, long-integrated representatives from the neighbouring province of Manitoba was very marked. For one thing, they were all able to speak English; for the others it meant the tedious process of translation to both Cree and Ojibwa, and it was only too obvious that much was lost in the translation sometimes, for a question would be asked and an answer given, then ten minutes later someone would ask the identical question, only phrased somewhat differently. And I wondered as I sat there, why, if the department or the government or whoever it was had taken so much trouble with this book *Choosing a Path*, had they not taken the trouble to translate it into Cree and Ojibwa? I know that across the great length and breadth of our country there is a multiplicity of dialects — but even ten or twenty translations would have helped, and could not have been beyond the bounds of feasibility, for something of such importance. And I thought too that the remote bands should have been visited long before by a patient lawyer, or at least some form of ombudsman, so that the people would thoroughly understand all the ramifications of these issues that were being raised today.

They were well aware of the gravity of their answers, how their people's futures might be altered by them, but coming from the slow, slow tempo of the reserve to this meeting in the city, and suddenly facing the decisions of change, and the worry of doing the right thing for the generations ahead, soon had them harassed into speeches that began with "wait, wait, let us consider it further," while the activists and sophisticates pulled them ever faster and further into the mire of confusion. And, "Those behind cried 'Forward!' And those before cried 'Back!' " — only the other way round.

And when I left I thought of them flying back to places like Big Trout and Pekangicum, Casabonika and Sandy to report to their people and try and clarify issues that must still appear muddied even to them. I would have liked to have said to them that they were returning to something infinitely enviable, and to tell their people that whatever the outcome of these conferences, whatever the changes that lay ahead, or the confusions of the outside world, never to forget that they had something of inalterable, priceless security in this background of themselves. For I think that soon there will be no territory more valuable than "land reserved for the exclusive use of its aboriginal people." It will be a constant world within a world where "all is flux and nothing stands still," and in a future of emergence and integration it will be a place to go forth from, but a place that is always there to return to for the stability and security and refreshment that comes of being among one's own people. Some may go forth and never feel the need or the urge to return, some may find that they depend upon it less and less; some may even find that its greatest benefit lies in its disparaging contrast to the world outside, and there will always be some who cannot exist without it — but it will always be there, as long as the rocks remain and the rivers run, as we heard so often quoted that afternoon. One day they will use their reserves as the

Mohawks of Cauchnawaga use theirs now — leaving it to work in Montreal, or to follow the trades of steeplejack and high rigger, at which they are unequalled, in cities all over the North American continent, whole families leaving to live a totally integrated city life, earning the highest wages, yet returning to Cauchnawaga between jobs to recharge themselves within the culture and pace of life of their own people and background.

As an immigrant perhaps I understand the value of such a sanctuary more deeply than the more solidly rooted Canadian. I love the land of my adoption, yet when I return to my native land I feel immediately enfolded by custom and dictate; one merges rightfully into a background, there is no need to explain who or why one is, no need for justification, apology or pretence — it is already known; one is an aboriginal once more, and the soil is full of our bones.

And so I would have liked to have said, too, that there is another kind of enviable value to reserved land, for we white people who came to this land are as dispossessed of the soil that formed us or our forebears as they once were. And perhaps this is why, because of our restless unconscious search for another protective background, we are becoming more and more nomadic, with our ever-proliferating trailers and tents and mobile homes, our wistful emulation in outdoor barbecues and tanning oils, forever searching for that idyllic overnight — or over-lifetime — site away from the "all" of our own civilisation. Forever without, having slaved for our "fifty weeks in hopes of living like the Indians for two," looking over the invisible palisades that we ourselves put up so many years ago, we will enviously behold a Utopian campsite, a sanctuary, an oasis in an arid troubled world into which only the Indian people may enter and find peace and refreshment.

Lastly, I would have liked to have said to those chiefs and counsellors flying back to the reality of their own world — tell your people, when they come, to bring with them some of the warmth and sharing and humour, the dignity and endurance that has kept them so proudly together throughout the centuries, so that we others may share something of their heritage on common ground, without reserve, and be strengthened as a nation.